ANSWERING
THE CALL

BEYOND
PUBLISHING

New York | Los Angeles | London | Sydney

10 9 8 7 6 5 4 3 2 1 ISBN 978-0-9987292-1-3

TABLE OF CONTENTS

ENDORSEMENTS

"If you want to know what it looks like to understand and respond to the call of full-time ministry, you need to read this book. Ron gets it. He lives it. He whole-heartedly believes in the God of the impossible. His clear understanding of Scripture and godly tenacity has helped establish countless ministries and plant dozens of churches around the world. His passion for New York City – ever since the founding of Every Nation New York in the wake of 9/11 – has inspired and changed many lives. I praise the Lord for people like Ron and am happy to call him a friend."

Luis Palau, *International Evangelist*

"Ron Lewis has helped more young people answer the Call to ministry than anybody I know. These principles will guide you confidently into the purposes of God."

Dr. Rice Broocks, *Co-founder, Every Nation,*
Author of God's Not Dead and Man, Myth, Messiah

"I was saved long before I started walking the Christian walk. When I really realized the gift I had been given, I felt I needed to take a stand, yet had no idea how to take my years of coaching and helping others to the next level. Pastor Ron and this book helped give me the instruction I needed to fulfill my purpose and help others find theirs. It is a must-read if you want to make a difference in the Kingdom!"

Bill Lam, *10X ACC Coach of the Year (at UNC),*
National Coach of the Year

"Answering the Call has been a valuable resource for our campus ministry. It's helped hundreds of individuals discern God's direction for their lives. It strikes the perfect balance between presenting the realities and challenges of vocational ministry while inspiring faith in the God who made the call to begin with. While its focus is on ministry, it also honors and respects the call into all sectors of society, including the marketplace. Pastor Ron Lewis shares generously from the highs and lows of experience and those of others to share the reality of what answering the call looks like."

Joseph Bonifacio, Director,
Every Nation Campus – Philippines

"Ron Lewis captures nearly every angle of what it means to serve God. This book will act as a mentor as you sift through your options and listen to what God is saying to you through your gifts and passions. I am sure you will hear His voice as you read."

Dr. Tim Elmore, Founder, GrowingLeaders.com

"In the modern church, ministry is often tragically reduced to a career, instead of a calling. In Answering the Call, Ron Lewis offers critical wisdom to this important distinction. Ron is a seasoned voice with an authority that only comes having lived out the message before many. I'm thankful for his leadership and friendship!"

Dominic Russo, Visionary, 1Nation1Day;
Founder, Missions.Me

"Ron has penned a masterpiece of sound judgment, clear reasoning, and fatherly love. This book is a lighthouse to many, that they may not crash their new-found faith against the rocks of life, but that they navigate safely to shore and live out their life's calling as a full-time minister of the gospel of Jesus Christ."

Olajide Pariola, Regional Director,
Every Nation Campus – Southern Africa

"This book gives a seasoned interpretation for discerning God's still, small voice and a clear roadmap for practically answering that call to ministry. I love handing this book individuals who are looking to lay hold of that for which Jesus laid hold of them."

Rollan Fisher, Church Planter and Founding Pastor,
Second City Chicago

"Pastor Ron Lewis has penned a practical, inspired, and easy-to-read occupational pathway for every student desiring to know the will of God for her or his life."

"Answering the Call is a must-read for every believer of every level. Pastor Ron has not only been a mentor, but has also helped me realize my call."

"This down-to-earth guide is full of nuggets of wisdom from Ron's years of hands-on ministry experience. By gleaning from his insights, you will, undoubtedly, gain clarity on how God desires to minister through you. A 'must-read' both for those in ministry and those seeking direction for their lives."

"It has been my privilege to count Ron Lewis as a friend for many years. *Answering the Call* is a clear reflection of his evident passion for developing others. Both compassionate and challenging, Ron demonstrates a rare ability to recognize the gifts of others and reveal how those gifts fit into God's creative and masterful plan. *Answering the Call* is a roadmap to discovery for any Christian who desires to find their true calling in Christ."

"Answering the Call is a down-to-earth book that will encourage and enlighten anyone considering full-time ministry. Ron Lewis uses his personal life adventures and the stories of others to explore the call many feel on their lives. It is a great, practical tool for anyone weighing the costs of full-time ministry."

"This book gives a refreshing perspective on the call to ministry that infuses us with both great hope and sobriety. May we all, with sobriety and optimism, consider God's call and respond to it."

Reggie Roberson, Senior Associate Pastor,
King's Park International Church;
Campus Ministry Director, Duke University and North Carolina
Central

"Ron Lewis has devoted much of his life to fulfilling Jesus' strategy of sending ministers into God's harvest. Answering the Call is a biblically based, practical guide for those who want to reach their world with the gospel. This is a much-needed book in our European context."

Tom Jackson, Founder,
Centre for European Church Planting

"As a campus missionary for the past 15 years, I have needed a tool to help students biblically and practically understand what it means to be called into full-time ministry. This book is a tool that answers those questions. I highly recommend it to any person wrestling with the idea of going into ministry."

Nicholas Jones, North American Director,
Every Nation Campus

"*Answering the Call* is the most practical resource I have ever seen to help young people discern the call of Jesus on their life. Our campus ministry at UNC-Chapel Hill has helped release over 100 missionaries into God's harvest field over the years and the content from this book has played a critical role in that happening. Each page helps answer specific questions in a faith-filled and action-oriented way."

Jason McDaniel, Mid-Atlantic Director, Every Nation Campus

"After being a pre-med student and philosophy major at Duke University, I identified with Pastor Ron and answered God's call to ministry in my life. This book is a practical how-to guide on responding to God's call to full-time ministry and will bring the clarity you need to help make this critical decision."

Bryan Scott, Campus Pastor,
Columbia University and New York University

"After a long season of disappointment and seeming silence in my calling, Ron Lewis took me by the hand and walked me back to my burning bush. Whether you are just beginning to feel the rumblings of God's call in your life or are deeply wading through life's mush to resurrect it, Ron's wisdom, discernment, and simplicity in *Answering the Call* will bring clarity to you, too, in discovering the sweet-spot of your calling."

Veronica Karaman, *Golf Professional,*
Personal Leadership Coach, 1989 U.S. Open Participant

ACKNOWELDGEMENTS

I would like to thank and acknowledge the following people and groups for their contributions, stories, or efforts which made this book possible: Dr. Rice Broocks, Pastor Jim Laffoon, Pastor KC and Shih Chia, Simon Suh, Steve Hollander, Harold Bredeson, Pastor Jeff and Anna Bullock, Mike Watkins, Mart Green, Gene Mack, Tom Jackson, Whitney Miller, Eric Syfrett, Chris Berg, Taylor Stewart, Gerard Picco, David Tang, Nick Jones, Steve Murrell, Kara Reed Waddell, Carlos Antonio, Jed Walker, Galen Jernigan, King's Park International Church, Every Nation Church New York City, Every Nation Campus, the many campus ministers of North Carolina, my sons Nathan, Christian, Jordan, Johnluke, my dear wife Lynette, and my publisher Michael Butler along with his gracious team.

FORWARD
BY JIM LAFFOON

I have had the privilege of being Ron Lewis' friend and co-laborer for over three decades. We have worked together in churches throughout the United States and around the world. From our earliest days together, I have seen Ron cultivate an atmosphere wherein young men and women clearly hear the call to full-time gos-pel ministry. Whether it has been through King's Park International Church, the churches he has launched, the Campus Harvest Student Conference, or our larger Every Nation family, we have seen hundreds and thousands of young people called into ministry.

Through King's Park, approximately 100 churches have been planted, and over 500 students and young people have answered the call to full-time ministry. Through our Every Nation student conferences, I have watched hundreds of students give their lives to God through full-time ministry by serving as campus ministers, church planters, pastors, and missionaries. Although it is often a challenging road from the call to its fruition, books like this are wisdom and help as young people navigate this calling. It's not for the faint of heart.

Ron's passion to support those who have been called into vocational ministry has never waned. King's Park has allocated millions of dollars to advance God's kingdom through campus ministry, church planting, and missions—both in the United States and abroad. Ron has also spent untold hours mentoring young people who have been called into ministry.

Although Ron has preached in conferences and churches around the world, he would much rather stand before a group of passionate young people who desire to change the world. This book, Answering the Call, is more than just an inspirational challenge to find and fulfill God's calling. It is a practical handbook on how to respond to that call and provides many answers to the most frequent questions people have regarding this topic. Whether you are wrestling with a sense of God's calling in your own life, helping others to answer God's call for their lives, or a parent of a person who may be called of God, this book is for you.

Yours for the mobilization of another generation of Christian workers,

Jim Laffoon
Sr. Teaching Minister
Every Nation Churches and Ministries

DEDICATION

This book is dedicated to those who are sensing the call of God as they enter a deep desire to follow Jesus, pick up their cross, and sur-render all for His glory.

It is for those who know well they have been crucified with Christ, their life is not their own, they cannot escape this call any more than they can escape life itself.

You are one whose heart has stirred you for some time. You have had moments where you felt His nearness. You have heard His voice and are yearning to do His will.

You have been both blessed and bothered by the still small voice of God. You consider every earthly gain secondary to the call— your academic advances, your future careers, and your potential wealth. Your deepest longings in life have been eclipsed by your greater passion to follow Him and advance His kingdom.

You've abandoned all other measurements to be measured by one thing alone: Did you chase and grasp what your Father has called you to? This book is dedicated to you. Go forward and don't look back. Press on to take hold of your calling.

Christ has taken hold of you, so that you will take hold of it. Heaven
and earth are waiting for you...

INTRODUCTION

"I press on to take hold of that for which
Christ Jesus took hold of me."
Philippians 3:12

1982. A hot August day at the University of North Carolina at Chapel Hill.

It was my first day in full-time ministry. I did not have much to work with. I had no paycheck. No support team. No job description. No seminary degree. No agenda to follow. But, what I had was enough. I had been apprehended by God. I had a vision and a mission.

All I owned—including my recent rolled-up diploma—was in the back seat of my broken-down Pontiac. I could pick the lint off the back of my pants, thanks to the rips in the padded driver's seat. It was embarrassing, but I didn't care. I was on a mission from God.

I will never forget that first day. I was on campus as students were moving in to their dorms for the new school year. The task was massive and the opportunities were endless, but I had to start somewhere. Like anyone in this position, I wanted to give myself the best chance at some early success.

Another campus minister invited me to visit a student who had showed a little interest in the things of God. I thought she would welcome a young, energetic, vibrant campus evangelist who stopped by to visit. It seemed like a safe way to start my new "career" as a campus missionary.

The student turned out to be a passionate feminist from the Northeast. She was brilliant and persuasive. I was prepared to discuss all kinds of issues and ideas, including what it means to have a relationship with God. Too bad we never got there. It turns out, like me, she had a Jewish upbringing.

Initially, I thought that would help. But it didn't. Not even a little bit.

She was offended that someone sharing her heritage would show up at her dorm wanting to talk about Jesus. She was infuriated. She didn't want to debate; she wanted to fight. I was so repulsive to her that she couldn't help but unload on me. She cussed me out and dropped several "colorful" words. She said I was a traitor. She fumed until all I could do was silently pray for the Rapture to come.

It was a humble beginning, but it is what I remember about that first day. No new friends made. No "applauding angels." No "souls saved." Though it did not feel like it at the time, it was a fitting way to start my calling as a minister. Obeying God and serving Him as a full-time minister will not save you from difficult days. In fact, it will probably lead you straight into them.

It happened to Jesus when He obeyed His Father and ministered to the people in His day. It happened to the twelve apostles who followed Jesus into a life of ministry. And it has happened to almost everyone else who has been willing to serve God in a full-time vocation since.

That day was a turning point for me. In my frustration and discouragement, I told God I believed in my calling. I told God I believed in His choice for my calling. I believed that this is what He wanted me to do and that wherever this road would take me, I would tell the world.

In my youthful immaturity I said, "Okay, God, whatever happens, good or bad, I'm going to tell everyone. If I go broke, I'll tell everyone—I'll shout it from the rooftops. If I die on the mission field of starvation, if I get cussed out every day, whatever it looks like, this is going to be our story together."

Here I am over thirty-five years later, sharing the story of God and what has happened since I answered His call. After all these years, I want the world to know that the Lord has been faithful. Serving God as a full-time minister has been one of the greatest joys and privileges I have known. I have not been perfect, but I have been faithful to the call He so graciously has given me.

Now, my passion is to help you sort through your specific calling. We are all called to God, but we have different callings on our lives. It might mean that you decide God has called you to full-time vocational ministry, or it might mean God has called you to be a light in the marketplace. Either way, His callings are good.

The fact you are reading this today tells me you are in the process of discovering what He has in store for you. My prayer for you is whether you serve God in full-time ministry or from another profession, you realize He has called each of us to be ministers, regardless of our work.[1]
This book is specifically written to bring greater understanding into what it means to serve in professional ministry, as a career and full-time vocation. Along the way, many of us who have a relationship with Jesus wonder if this is for us, if we would be willing to say "yes" if He called us to do it.

It certainly is not for everyone, but, if it is for you, I want to encourage you: God will come through for you! It will be challenging and, at times, deeply disappointing, but, if you are doing this for Him, you are in for the adventure of a lifetime.

---

[1] 2 Timothy 1:9

1

WHAT IS FULL-TIME MINISTRY?

" 'Come follow me,' Jesus said, 'and I will send you out to fish for people.'
At once, they left their nets and followed him."
Matthew 4:19-20

What do you think of when you hear the phrase, "full-time ministry?" Maybe you think of a man in a collar or flowing robes, a preacher on TV, or a missionary in the bush of Africa, the frozen tundra of Siberia, or the jungles of the Amazon. Perhaps you think of a campus minister who has helped you get to know Jesus in a personal way.

To a degree, these can all be examples of full-time ministry. From here on, when I use the phrase "full-time ministry," I am mindful that all ministry— in every sphere of life—is a full-time calling. However, for the sake of clarity in this book, when I refer to full-time ministry, I am referring to a man or woman whose primary occupation is gospel ministry and all it entails.[2] Full-time ministry is a job, a vocation, and a career, but, as we will see in the next few chapters, it is so much more.

This subject is often misunderstood and usually brings with it a handful of questions:

- Does God want you to go into full-time ministry? (Chapter 2)
- What is the real difference between a Christian who works a "secular job" and a full-time minister? (Chapter 3)
- Does it please God more if you are a full-time minister? (Chapter 3)
- If I go into ministry, where do I begin? (Chapter 5)
- What will it cost me to follow Jesus into full-time ministry? (Chapter 7)

---

[2]Gospel ministry includes: preaching the gospel, making disciples, church work, humanitarian work, social justice, and other aspects of the whole gospel of Christ.

- How can I be paid for doing Christian ministry? (Chapter 9)

You may have more questions than the few listed here, but, together we will get to the bottom of this issue and understand how God wants us to think about all these things. Let us start with the first one: *Does God want you to be in full-time ministry?*

After more than 35 years of asking and fielding this question, I have concluded that all believers in Christ should be ministers, but only those who are called and qualified should go into the ministry as a full-time vocation. 2 Timothy 1:9 says that God saved us *and* gave us a holy calling. This holy calling is different for all of us. But it can be summed up in one four-letter word: work.

The Bible has a lot to say about work. One of the first things it teaches about God is that He, Himself, works.

And, like in so many other ways, God calls us to be like Him. He created us to work, too. In fact, in Genesis 2, before God gave Adam a wife, He called him to work in cultivating and tending the garden of Eden.

Throughout Scripture, there is a clear sense that God created us with a specific plan in mind, but, in most cases, the Bible talks more about how we should work than what our specific job should be. Work is a part of how God orders everything. He said we are to work six days and rest one, not the other way around (wouldn't that have been nice?). Work was a part of life before sin entered the world. It is a facet of being like God.

The Apostle Paul—who wrote most of the New Testament—had a lot to say about this. He wrote repeatedly of his own hard work.[3] He said that we are God's handiwork,[4] created for "good works" that He prepared for us in advance. He encouraged the early Christians to honor hard work.[5] He said that followers of Christ should not steal but should work so that they could

---

[3] For starters, look at 1 Corinthians 4:12 and 2 Corinthians 6:5.

[4] This beautiful metaphor comes from Ephesians 2:10. The word translated as "handiwork" is the same Greek word that means "poem." Paul is saying that you are God's creative expression, His living poem.

[5] He strongly urges this in Romans 16:12 and 1 Thessalonians 5:12. It is clear that this was characteristic of how Paul thought ministry should be done, and he believed just as strongly that this should be recognized and honored with gratitude by those who were receiving this ministry.

share with others.[6] He even said that if you do not work, you should not eat.[7]

Paul truly helps us value all work in his letter to the Colossians. In Chapter 3, he writes instructions to servants who are doing difficult manual labor. They were struggling to discover how following Christ could transform their behavior on the job. "Whatever you do, work at it with all your heart, as working for the Lord, not human masters, since you know that you will receive an inheritance from the Lord as a reward. It is the Lord Christ you are serving." (Colossians 3:23-24)

According to Paul, there is no such thing as a "secular" job. All work is sacred, if it is done out of obedience and service to God. Author and thinker Dr. Os Guiness undergirds this concept in *The Call*: "In 1522, Luther declared that God and the angels smile when a man changes a diaper. William Tyndale wrote that, if our desire is to please God, pouring water, washing dishes, cobbling shoes, and preaching the Word 'is all one.'"[8]

Are you waiting tables or working an espresso machine? If you do it for God, it is holy. Perhaps, you are doing data entry in a cubicle, building websites, or auditioning for a Broadway show. With the right heart, it is a beautiful sacrifice that will receive a reward. It is the heart of the worker toward the One whom they are serving that makes a job holy.

Think of it this way: the Bible tells us that until He went to be baptized by John and started His ministry at age thirty, Jesus was a carpenter in His hometown of Nazareth. His Father loved Him. He was perfectly obedient. He was right where God wanted Him to be.

The same Jesus who experienced incredible intimacy and relationship with God as seen throughout the gospels was pounding nails and building things. Whether He was a carpenter or a full-time minister, the issue was His heart. He did what God called Him to do, whether it was sawing wood or preaching and healing the sick. He served different roles at different times, but His heart longed to be close to God every step of the way.

---

[6] Ephesians 4:28
[7] 2 Thessalonians 3:10
[8] Os Guiness, The Call, W Publishing Group: Nashville, TN, p. 34.

Here is the point: God wants us all to obey, to work hard, and to do our job, whatever it is, as a service to Him. The kingdom of God has a unique place and role for every member of the body of Christ. All of us are responsible to be faithful with what God has called us to do, without comparing it to everyone else. This is our ministry. It is the way that all followers of Christ contribute to the mission of God.

What makes the calling of full-time ministry different is that responding in obedience can lead us to leave our current endeavor and assume the occupation of ministry full-time.

History and Scripture are replete with examples of people who "left their nets and followed Him."

Moses was working the fields for his father-in-law, Jethro, when God called him to go to Pharaoh.[9] Elisha gave up a fortune of oxen when God called him to train under Elijah, in order to become a prophet.[10] Amos was a shepherd.[11] Jesus was a carpenter.[12] Simon, Andrew, James, and John were fishermen.[13] Matthew was an ignoble tax collector.[14] Saul of Tarsus was a lawyer.[15] God called all of them out of their vocation to follow Him into ministry.

Full-time vocational ministry is a calling that requires character and obedience to the Lord. Fortunately, He's still calling people today. The work of the kingdom of God must go on.

You may be working a job, wondering how your day-to-day responsibilities have anything to do with God's redemptive plans for the world. As Paul wrote, you do not have to quit your job for it to be a service to God and contribute to His mission.

---

[9] Exodus 3:1
[10] 1 Kings 19:19
[11] Amos 7:14
[12] Mark 6:3
[13] Matthew 4:18-21
[14] Matthew 10:3
[15] Philippians 3:4-6 says that, regarding the law, Paul was a Pharisee. A Pharisee was not a priest nor a minister; he was an expert of the law.

At the same time, what if God *does* call you, as He called so many before, to leave your current job or career path to serve Him full-time in the ministry? What if today He calls you to leave your "nets" as Peter, James, and John did? How would a calling like this happen? How would you know?

2

HOW DO I KNOW
IF I'M CALLED?

"But even before I was born, god chose me and called me by His marvelous grace. then it pleased Him to reveal his Son to me so that I would proclaim the Good News about Jesus . . ."
Galatians 1:15-16 (NLT)

God has not called everyone to be a full-time vocational minister, but all of us should be ministering with the entirety of our lives. In our homes, offices, at the grocery store, at the gym, in every area of our lives, we never let go of the mission of God. We are always contributing our part in fulfilling our role for God's mission on earth.

However, there is clear precedent in both the Old and New Testaments for full-time ministry, as we have previously defined it.

When God set out to restore His relationship with all of mankind, He started with one man and his family.[16] Over time, that man and his family grew, from a clan to a nation, to be the twelve tribes of Israel..

In his sovereignty, God chose the Israelites to be His people on earth. Out of His love and desire to have a special relationship with them, He gave the law, His covenants, and His promises, so they would show to all the nations what it meant to be the people of God.

Part of His plan in setting them apart was to divide them into twelve distinct tribes. Each tribe was a part of the larger nation, but they also had their own unique role. You may recall that Jesus was of the Tribe of Judah, which is

---

[16] That man's name was Abram, which later became Abraham. You can find the story beginning in Genesis 11:27 and follow it through the rest of Scripture.

why He is called "the Lion of the Tribe of Judah." That was His family heritage.[17]

The Levites were one of the twelve tribes given a unique role. God chose this tribe to be His priests, to serve in the temple, and to be responsible for all the ministerial duties the law required. Though the Levites were different than the other tribes, they were still just one of the twelve with their own strengths and weaknesses. God created special arrangements in order that their basic needs would be provided for and so they could give their full time and attention to the person of the Lord and the service of His people.[18]

In the earliest days of the church, the apostles followed the spirit of this approach, though not the structure. When Jesus chose His disciples, they left their vocations to follow and serve Jesus full-time. They were not all Levites, and God did not choose them on the basis of their family line. He said they were given to Him by His Father.[19]

In Acts 6, through the preaching and ministry of "the twelve," the church experienced explosive growth. So many disciples were being added that some of the responsibilities were being overlooked. They gathered as a group and divided the work so that the twelve could give themselves full-time to "prayer and the ministry of the Word." Today, God is still calling people to give their time and attention to the work of the Lord, to prayer, and to the ministry of the Word.

It is not based on your family line. The presence or lack of a full-time minister in your family does not determine your calling. Unlike the original disciples, Jesus does not have to reveal Himself in person for you to follow Him into ministry. It may not be as simple as knowing your family history. It may not be as crystal clear as the Son of God in human form showing up at your job, calling you to follow Him. But the calling *does* happen. The often-mysterious nature of the call always carries with it the opportunity to draw closer to Him

---

[17] To be precise, the tribe of Judah was Joseph's heritage, because Jesus was born of a virgin, and the family line was always traced through the man. To learn more about Jesus as the Son of God and the second Adam, read Romans 5.

[18] 1 Deuteronomy 18:1-8

[19] John 6:37, 44, 45

Before explaining this calling any further, it is imperative to understand that our primary calling as a follower of Jesus is unto Him before being called unto anything else. Os Guinness explains: "first and foremost we are called to Someone (God), not to something (such as motherhood, politics, or teaching) or to somewhere (such as the inner city or Outer Mongolia)."[20] Although not the focus of this book, I must stress that the Caller, God our Father, is far more important than the calling. Without God, we will certainly make our calling—whatever it may be—an idol, and it could lead to ruin.

Our primary calling is unto God. Our secondary calling, the focus of this book, has to do with our specific purpose for His glory. Discerning this is important, as God knows best what we should be doing with our lives, and that a sense of calling should precede a career choice. For some of us, that is a calling into full-time vocational ministry.

How do you know if God is calling you into full-time ministry? I have found the following four aspects of the calling to be helpful.

1. THE CALL

The realization of calling is not always clear-cut. It rarely answers all the questions at once. Sometimes, it does not answer any. Most of the time, it is as unique as the person being called.

As mentioned,[21] with salvation comes a holy calling. No two are alike, though in a broad sense, we all are given the same one based on His grace. Once you experience the call to full-time ministry, you are never the same. Here is how it happened for me. *April 2016: "Do you love me? Feed my sheep"*

I will never forget my experience at Alexander Dorm at UNC in the early '80s. Michael Jordan was often in the headlines in Chapel Hill, but God was moving, and amazing things were happening off court, as well. Some of the students on my hall were giving their lives to Christ, and some whom I had written off as unreachable were asking me salvation and eternal life. Those were good times.

---

[20] Os Guinness, The Call, p. 31.
[21] I am referring again to 2 Timothy 1:9. By the end of the book, you'll have it memorized!

I would regularly read the Bible for hours at a time. One month, all I could focus on in Scripture was how the disciples would go out and preach. In Mark 16, it says they went out and preached everywhere and the Lord worked with them.[22] Jesus specifically called them to go out and preach. It was all I could see. It was as if every Scripture on preaching and teaching was speaking to me too. I felt that, like them, Jesus was calling me.

I was beginning to feel anxious about it. It was such a strange thought for me as a first-generation Christian[23] in my family. It was not long thereafter that I had a life-defining moment

I was on a Greyhound bus going from school in Chapel Hill to my hometown of Greensboro. In those days, it was common for students who wanted a quick trip home to jump on the bus line. It was quick and cheap, and you could study during the ride. At that point in my life, it was hard for me to study anything other than the Bible. On the bus, I pulled my Bible out of my backpack and continued to ponder all the Lord had been saying to me. Suddenly, something strange began to occur. I closed my eyes and really listened intently to the still, small voice.

Although the bus was filled with a variety of people, it was as if it was only me and the Invisible One. He was there, and I could hear Him so clearly inside my heart saying, "Get up, and tell these people your story."

I could not believe it, or, perhaps more accurately, I did not want to believe it. Not me! Oh no, this could not be the Lord. Does He not know I have to keep my reputation of being a nice, normal guy?

Vivid images of what might happen were racing through my mind. They would probably stone me, like Stephen. At the very least, they would want to tie me down. Worse yet, they might tie me down and throw me out the doors without slowing down. Maybe the bus driver would slam on the breaks, sending me flying out of his huge windshield in a bloody mess on Interstate 40. I began to wonder if this whole thing could be the voice of the devil. It quickly occurred to me that the devil is not interested in getting God's kids out of their seats and onto the front of the bus to share the love of Christ.

---

[22] Mark 16:20

[23] At that time, very few in my extended family were Christian.

I devised a backup plan. I told the Lord that I would obey the bus driver's rules. This seemed like a safe way out. Certainly, the driver would never allow anyone to get up and preach Christ on a Greyhound. I thought my spontaneous excuse out of answering the "divine squeeze" was clever: I would ask for the bus driver's permission, get denied, and quietly return to my seat.

I timidly walked to the front and said, "Excuse me, sir. My name is Ron Lewis. I am sure that you have rules about not letting people give talks on your bus, but I wanted to see if you would, by chance, let me share my story about how God changed my life and Jesus Christ became my Lord. I know you probably won't let me, but I thought I would just ask anyway."

As I waited, hoping he would reject me, I took a deep breath. What happened next would mark me forever. He smiled and said he had no objection. He then went on to explain he was a Pentecostal[24] Christian and would be praying for me as I spoke. He made it even easier by handing me his microphone, so my voice could be amplified through the entire bus!

God called my bluff and led me straight out of my comfort zone. All I lacked was a choir, because, for the next twenty-five minutes, we had a powerful church service. I preached while the bus driver silently prayed. And, glory to God, the people responded!

I invited people to repent of their sins and give their lives to Christ, and they responded all over the bus. Some people requested counsel. Others smiled. Everyone prayed and was encouraged. To my surprise, not one person had any issue or objection.

As the bus arrived in Greensboro, I rushed forward, so I could jump off first and stand at the bottom of the bus exit door. I was like the pastor at the greeting line of a church. The passengers exited the bus, shook my hand, hugged my neck, or sincerely thanked me. Everyone was smiling, because, for the previous hour, the joy of the Lord had taken over that bus. It was quite a moment. If I ever had any doubts about my call, they were gone.

I was consumed with the knowledge that people needed to be reached, the

---

[24] Pentecostal refers to a particular Christian, charismatic denomination.

poor helped, new churches planted, and all I could say was, "Yes, Lord!" The Scriptures on "preaching everywhere" were now in full revelation in my heart. My calling was being realized right in front of my eyes.

The call can come through unusual means, as it did for me. Other calls, as we shall read about later, could be characterized as a process, instead of an event or moment. For example:

God called Moses through a burning bush.[25]

Moses' brother, Aaron, was called through hearing about Moses' talk with God.[26]

Joseph was called through a series of mysterious dreams and the persecution of his brothers.[27]

Jesus appeared to Paul in a vision and spoke in an audible voice on the road to Damascus.[28]

Timothy was called through prophetic words and the leadership and spiritual upbringing he received from Paul.[29]

Augustine[30] was called in a garden by the voice of an unseen child.

Martin Luther[31] was saved and called through a terrifying lightning storm.

---

[25] You can find this story in Exodus 3.

[26] This story follows in Exodus 4.

[27] This happens in Genesis 37. Joseph's story is one of the longest in Genesis and continues until chapter 50.

[28] You can find this story in Acts 9. Remember, at this point, he was still known as Saul. God would later change his name, as a sign of a new beginning. 29 The prophetic words are referenced in 1 Timothy 1:18-19, and both of Paul's letters to Timothy are evidence of the mentoring role that he played in the life of this young leader.

[30] Widely recognized as one of the most significant theologians in church history, Augustine heard a child that he couldn't see say "tolle lege" which means "take up and read." He took it to mean the Bible, and, when he opened it randomly to Romans 13:13, he felt God was calling him to follow Him.

[31] Martin Luther is best remembered for his pivotal role in the Protestant Reformation and is one of the most important figures in Christian history.

John Wesley[32] was called during a storm at sea as he feared for his life.

John Newton, author of the hymn Amazing Grace, was called to ministry after attempting to reform the slave trade, of which he was once a part.

These callings are unique, but they share a single characteristic. When God called, the call was answered and obeyed.

2. DESIRE

At the risk of stating the obvious, at some point along the way, you need desire to do the work of the ministry.[33] Sometimes at a Christian conference or in a powerful moment in which many of your friends are feeling called to ministry, it is easy to get swept up in the moment. The call sounds impressive and it makes you feel holy, perhaps even spiritually strong.

In the long-run, the desire to do full-time ministry will not be enough. But, it can be a great place to start. Over time, the stress, pressure, adversity, and challenges of this assignment have a way of revealing motives and clarifying your call.

Keep in mind that there is nothing wrong with simply volunteering. Andy Stanley, the lead pastor of one of the largest churches in America, says that as intently as he wanted to minister full-time early in his life, he never felt truly called.[34] He asked his dad, Charles Stanley (also pastor of a large church), if someone had to be called to go into full-time ministry, or if it is enough to simply volunteer? *discipleship*

3/24/17: one zone w/ Lionel has been good so far

His dad thought it was fine just to begin as a volunteer, so that is exactly what Andy did. Before long, God confirmed his initial desire was truly a calling through the obvious gifts and ministry success that Andy experienced.

From the simple, small act of volunteering, his calling was confirmed, and

---

[32] John Wesley is most remembered as the founder of Methodism, for circuit-riding, for large outreach events, and a penchant for writing popular hymns.

[33] 1 Timothy 3:1 says "If someone aspires to be a church leader, he desires an honorable position." (NLT) The same holds true for full-time ministry.

[34] Andy shares this story on page 9 of the Introduction. Stanly, Andy. Communicating for A Change. Sisters, OR: Multnomah Press, 2006.

God used Andy to see thousands of lives changed. We can see from this story that sometimes, desire grows into calling.

Often, God uses <u>availability</u> over ability. When you are willing to simply volunteer and obey Him, He will be faithful to reveal the unique spot He has designed specifically for you. A willing heart is filled with possibility, because it is in motion and able to be led exactly where God leads. As the saying goes, "God doesn't call the equipped; <u>he equips the called</u>."

This reminds me of my dear friends, Jeff and Anna Bullock. Their story shows what can happen when you love God and are willing to follow His call. While attending North Carolina State University, Jeff became a Christian, and his life was never the same. After a few years of growing and maturing as a believer, he had a dream from God. In the dream, he was boarding a plane to Russia to start a new church. Interestingly enough, that same night, his pastor also had a dream of starting churches in the former Soviet Union. The dreams made him wonder if this is what God wanted him to do.

Within four months, a good friend Mike Watkins was ministering in Lviv, Ukraine (a university town of a million people on the eastern border of Ukraine). A short-term mission trip was soon to follow with Jeff leading the team, and, by the time the trip was over, a church had been launched.

As he returned to the United States with the rest of the team, Jeff had no idea that this trip had given him a glimpse of God's calling for his life. He wanted to lead other mission teams into Eastern Europe.

One afternoon, while lying on his sofa, he was overwhelmed by the presence of God. He had a deep sense that God was calling him to move to Ukraine, to serve God, love people, and build the church. He had never imagined living in Europe before, so this calling made it clear to him that it must, indeed, be his diving calling.

Immediately, he announced the "good news" to his wife, Anna. Good news to some isn't good news to all. She said, "Well . . . you can go without me!" Until she had heard from God as well, they decided to wait. Jeff did not want to arrive in Ukraine and have Anna angry with him for making her live in Eastern Europe. Anna's response to Jeff's call underscores an immovable boundary within a marriage that all decisions toward full-time ministry must have 100 percent agreement between a husband and wife.

A few months later, she realized this dream was not simply her husband's, but, rather, that it was God's purpose for their family. Today, in the wake of their calling, there are several churches in Ukraine, and a dynamic church in Krakow, Poland. The team is growing, and it is clear that there is no end in sight.

The desire within Jeff and Anna has been like the caboose on a train. It has *adopted* always been there, but it has never led way. Often, passion is espoused as the chief driver of calling. While it can and does fuel the flame, it is not enough and often falls short, in and of itself. When vision, character, and the Cross are present, the calling can be fulfilled.

Initially, moving to Ukraine was not Jeff and Anna's burning desire, but, when God called, they went

3. GIFTING BEYOND THE ORDINARY

If God calls, He also gives the gifts for the calling.

When athletes compete for a team, they are given the shoes, uniforms, and equipment they need to play. Soldiers are given a helmet, camouflage, armor, and a variety of weapons and tools necessary for success. In the same way, God gives gifts to His people.[35] These gifts help us fulfill the ministry we have been called to do. A divine calling, spiritual gifts, proven character, and acquired skills are non-negotiables for a ministry calling to be effective. Regarding the gifts, one may not be using them regularly early on, but it should be clear that the potential is there. With a call comes the grace and talents to fulfill it.

I have heard many young, passionate leaders assure me they are going to be the next mega-pastor like Rick Warren.[36] However, upon closer examination,

---

[35] You can see this idea developed in Ephesians 4:11-16 and 1 Peter 4:10. These gifts are given to serve the body of Christ and to accomplish the Great Commission.

[36] Rick Warren is the founding pastor of Saddleback Church in Southern California and author of The Purpose Driven Life. The church has regular weekend attendance of 22,000, and, according to Publisher's Weekly, the book has sold more than 30 million copies, perhaps making it the best-selling non-fiction hard-cover book in history.

many of these young dreamers have never led people to Christ or started a Bible study.

↳ start a group...

Maybe they feel certain their newly started non-profit organization will have the same global impact achieved by Mother Teresa or Scott Harrison.[37] This, too, seems out of place, when you consider the fact they have never even wiped a single runny nose serving in a church nursery.[38]

It is important to point out here that the need to demonstrate gifts is not the same thing as having talent. There are certain elements of ministry that someone with talent can be successful through their own abilities. A charismatic leader with excellent communication skills can draw a crowd and grow an organization, but God often builds His kingdom through His grace and the gifts He gives to us in our weakness.

↳ praying / spending time w/ God in preparation for a meeting

Moses struggled with a speech impediment, yet he led a congregation of several million through the Red Sea and the wilderness. The Apostle Thomas had his doubts, yet he was one of the Twelve and eventually became the apostle to India. Though many of us may know him as "doubting Thomas," he did not doubt for long.

Rahab may have been a prostitute, an unlikely candidate to be used of God. Yet, through her faith, God used her to help the Israelites inherit the promise. She is honored for her faith in Hebrews 11:31 and is found in the lineage of Jesus.[39]

Paul went so far as to call his weakness a gift, because it helped him not to confuse his role in the work of God. Though he was a significant leader who regularly performed miracles, was divinely inspired to write Scripture, and was the primary authority in discipline and conflict management in the early church, he was, above all, a servant.[40]

Although Paul had a great background with strong credentials and is

---

[37] Scott Harrison is the founder of Charity Water, which has provided clean water to millions of people around the world.

[38] Paul describes this paradox and the tension between our weakness and God's strength in several places. Check out chapter 4 in both 1 and 2 Corinthians.

[39] Matthew 1:5

[40] 1 Corinthians 4:1

considered by many to be one of the great minds of history, he did not lead on the basis of talent or intellect. When he considered his own shortcomings and the enormity of the task he was attempting, his only chance for success was to trust in God's strength working in his weakness and to be a good steward[41] of what God had entrusted to him.

In the long-run, in order for lives to be transformed, the sick to be healed, the captive to be set free, the gospel to be preached in power and not just persuasion, it takes God's grace working through the gifts He has given those servants who have demonstrated great character and humility before the Lord.

If you think God has given you a gift in an area of ministry, volunteer to serve in that area. See if God's grace is there working on your behalf. Do you enjoy it? Are you good at it? Has anyone ever commented on your gift in that area? If so, these can be helpful clues that will lead you to understand the gifts God has given you. *possible gifts: intercession, prayer in general, observant, sensitive*

4. CONFIRMATION

When God is leading someone into full-time ministry through a real calling, a growing desire, and the evidence and operation of necessary gifts, the confirmation will always come. Confirmation is a clear stamp of approval. It is God's endorsement. It is not always loud and dramatic, but it always acknowledges and points to God, and not necessarily the minister. Every person in the Bible who received a call to serve the Lord full-time also received a confirmation of that calling from the Lord and His people.

For the Levites, it was without question. It had been their birthright from the time Jacob blessed his son, Levi. For the Old Testament prophets, it was the moment when they obeyed and spoke the Word of the Lord. Their position as God's ministers was not always immediately obvious; sometimes God asked prophets to do crazy things that the people did not understand.[42] But,

---

[41] A steward was the manager of the household, and that term applies to the management of responsibilities, based on the commissioning of the one in authority. It is a concept used throughout Scripture. Jesus used it on several occasions, including as a dividing line in a difficult parable in Luke 12:35-48.

[42] He told Jeremiah that the people would fight him and try to kill him when he spoke, but He would rescue them. He told and showed Ezekiel so many crazy things I can't believe he actually wrote them down to show anybody else. He told Hosea to marry a prostitute! He told Jonah to go to the biggest, scariest city there was and preach against it. This list could go on and on, but God confirmed His words and the people He gave them, too.

when they obeyed, God confirmed them as His true prophets as their words came to pass.[43]

When Jesus first sent out His followers to do the work of the ministry, He gave them a serious challenge. Take nothing with you, preach the kingdom, heal the sick, and drive out demons. Though they had seen Him do it, they must have thought, "There is NO way we can do this ourselves." When they went, however, God removed the "no" and made the way. He confirmed their obedience with the demonstration of His power. They came back to Jesus and gave the glowing report of many breakthroughs: "Lord, even the demons are subject to us in your name." [44] Jesus' authority was extended and replicated through them serving as strong confirmation.

Just a few years later, the church was worshipping and praying in Antioch when the Spirit said, "Set apart for me Barnabas and Saul for the work to which I have called them."[45] How the Spirit spoke this, we do not know. What we *do* know is that this was a major confirmation for a missionary team to be set apart to reach all of Europe with the gospel. God is still confirming callings today.

He did it for me whenever I obeyed in my weakness. Each time, He met me with His strength. As I mustered up the faith and courage to step out in preaching the Bible, often to my surprise, people responded. Lives were transformed and men and women came into supernatural, loving relationships with God through the person of Christ and the power of the Holy Spirit.

Has God called you? Do you have the desire to obey God in this call? Has He given the gifts that you need to do what you believe you are called to do? Have you and others around you seen His power confirming you as you have obeyed and responded to the call?

If you are answering yes to all of, or even some of, these questions, then, in all likelihood, you are wrestling through the process of a call of God to full-time service. Using these questions as a checklist is incredibly important

---

[43] Samuel's confirmation in 1 Samuel 3:20 is a great example.

[44] You will find this quote in Luke 10:17, and the full story in Luke 10:1-24.

[45] Acts 13:2

in the process of working through your potential call to full-time ministry. Take some time now to stop and pray through them. Seek proven, godly counsel. *Please do not attempt this without qualified council and input.* When you are ready, come back to read on.

✓ 1. The Call
✓ 2. Desire
3. Gifting Beyond the Ordinary
4. Confirmation

2. Desire
shouldn't everyone have this desire?
to preach gospel & make disciples
do I actually have this desire?
- I have a desire to lay hands on people (strangers)
- I have a desire to see people accept Christ as Savior and Lord
- I have a desire to see healing for the sick
- I desire for God's shalom to rest in this place (where I live) Cambridge
- I desire to help out w/ discipleship; specifically just being there to go through questions/scripture together
- I have a desire to open up spaces for God's Holy Spirit to move

3. Gifting
Not sure what my gifting is, but preparing for ministry via praying is something that works well for me
→ Though I do have to set aside that time before meeting up w/ people

4. Confirmation
? unsure if there has been any so far

3
MINISTRY IN THE MARKETPLACE

"Instead, speaking the truth in love, we will in all things grow up into him who is the head, that is, Christ. From him the whole body, joined and held together by every supporting ligament, grows and builds itself up in love, ***as each part does its work . . ."***
Ephesians 4:15, 16

Not all of us can be NFL[46] quarterbacks. If fans know only one player on a football team, it is the quarterback. When kids go out to play, they pretend they are quarterbacks. Just take a quick look at the jerseys worn in stadiums, and you will be able to see how the pretending goes on into adulthood.

As recognizable as a quarterback is, he is helpless without linemen to protect him. The Academy Award-winning movie, *Blindside,* portrayed that well. He also needs a receiver to throw to and a running back to take the hand-off. He needs a defense to keep the other team from scoring. He needs coaches to create and teach plays, and a trainer to keep him strong and in shape. He needs administrators (the front office) to account for all the details that keep the team running.

While the quarterback may get much of the glory, he is also the one who takes vicious hits that he cannot see coming. When the team struggles, he is the first guy to get booed by his own supporters, while his replacement becomes the most popular guy on the team. It is a good thing we are not all quarterbacks.

Sometimes, it is the same with pastors and full-time ministers. When you think of a large church, you often think of the pastors. Obviously, the goals, values, and priorities of quarterbacks and ministers are vast in their

---

[46] The "NFL" is the National Football League, and it is the most popular and successful sport in America.

differences, but, just like a quarterback, their success is dependent on a much larger team. A team can only become great when every member embraces and excels in their individual role.

Though he never saw a quarterback in his lifetime, Paul understood this concept well.[47] He realized that if the people of God were going to fulfill God's mission, they would have to become a great team

In Ephesians 4, he writes how God created different roles in the church, so that the people could be equipped to serve the Body of Christ. As the body becomes like Jesus (the head), it will become strong and grow in love. When did he say this would happen? As "each part does its work."[48]

All of us have work to do, a part that only we can play. Remember, full-time ministers are not the only ones who are called. Everyone has a calling,[49] and, as we discover what that is, we should give ourselves to it with all our abilities, gifts, and passion.

I have a close friend in New York who was the president of a company on Park Avenue. He has a successful business in commercial real estate, but his real passion is to lead people to Jesus. He appears to be entirely effortless in his passion. Before he comes to our church services on Sunday mornings, he regularly stops by Starbucks for a cup of coffee and the chance to share the love of God.

Recently, he wanted to encourage the barista,[50] so, instead of just saying "Thank you," when she gave him his latte, he told her, "You're such a blessing. God loves you so much." Then, he asked her if he could pray for her. She said yes, and, when he finished praying, he was surprised to discover that many of the other coffee-drinkers in the crowded Starbucks had bowed their heads and prayed along with him.

This is probably not what comes to mind when you think of daily life in midtown Manhattan, but it would not be an exaggeration to say that this

---

[47] I think he would have loved football, because he regularly used athletic metaphors.

[48] Ephesians 4:16

[49] Paul expands on this concept in his second letter to Timothy (2 Timothy 1:9).

[50] "Barista" is the fancy name for someone who works an espresso machine.

is a near-daily experience for my friend. My friend often referred to his calling as a "marketplace ministry,"[51] to excel in evangelism and excel in the workplace.

It could be easy to conclude that, because he is effortless at leading people to Jesus, my friend should quit his job and go into full-time ministry. But, if he did, who would be in the business meetings, interacting with executives and leaders who never set foot in church? What would happen to the resources that his job generates for the kingdom of God? How could a pastor possibly do this same type of ministry? He cannot, because these doors are uniquely open to my friend.

Remember, there is no secular and sacred divide in work and calling. Every sphere of society belongs to God.[52] As theologian Abraham Kuyper said years ago, "There is not a square inch in the whole domain of our human existence over which Christ, who is sovereign over all, does not cry: Mine!"

When you are on a team where each person executes their role, there is a gratitude and camaraderie that you feel just for being on the team. When I work with people like my friend in New York and so many others who are called to minister in their daily lives, I am very aware that if all I did was follow up on their fruit, my job would be fulfilling.

The dynamics between full-time ministers and those ministering in the marketplace should be a beautiful partnership. Whenever people see a great team, they are attracted to it. As those following their calling in business pursue God's mission, it creates more work and need for their full-time ministry teammates. And, as the minister does his or her work, the effects should be felt in every area of marketplace life. That is how a team works; even when you cannot see it, the success of one hinges on the success of the other.

The Bible is filled with people who were not full-time ministers, those God used to do amazing things and accomplish His mission. Nehemiah was a

---

[51] Colossians 1:6 tells us that all things have been created by Him (Jesus) and for Him. Jesus is Lord over everything.

[52] Colossians 1:6 tells us that all things have been created by Him (Jesus) and for Him. Jesus is Lord over everything.

cup-bearer to the king. Abraham was a landowner and farmer. Daniel was a political consultant. Joseph was a manager and governor. Ruth was a servant. Deborah was a national leader. Esther was queen in an ungodly nation.

Jesus called twelve to follow Him full-time, but there were plenty He reached, loved, and ministered to that He sent right back to their marketplace work. Jesus healed the servant of a Roman Centurion.[53] Roman soldiers were despised, because of their regular cruelty to and abuse of the Jews, but Jesus made no attempt to call him out of his occupation.

Paul saw an opportunity to demonstrate the kingdom of God through the way that followers of Christ interacted, even in the most difficult relationship between slaves and masters.[54] He was by no means endorsing the institution of slavery, but he saw that particular component of the marketplace in desperate need of ministry. He was so committed to his role on the team that he even encouraged believers to pursue the call of the marketplace when it made the work of his own ministry even more challenging.[55]

A great example of the importance of marketplace ministry comes from the life of David Green, who came from a family with a long history of preachers. Although David Green received great pressure from his mother to be a full-time preacher of the gospel, he knew inside that full-time ministry was not his path. His five siblings have all responded to the call to go full-time, yet he could not. Years later, with a $600 start-up loan, he launched a home business that would change the world. Today, Hobby Lobby is a multi-billion-dollar industry that models biblical values in every aspect of their work and corporation.

In urban churches around the globe, many actors and models have come to Christ. Often, other young zealots insist that these new Christians need to leave their "dark and tempting" professions. There are times when that is the best advice; however, that is not my typical counsel. If God has placed them in this work, to walk away could be a mistake. Like all of us, they need to develop godly character and live a holy life, but the theaters and

---

[53] Luke 7:1-10
[54] Ephesians 6:5-9
[55] This is the subject of the amazing letter of Philemon.

runways of the world need salt and light, too. It might sound strange and even contradictory to discourage some from going into full-time ministry; however, God often leaves people in the place where they can honor Him and bear the most fruit.

Some people erroneously see the ministry as glamorous, the fast-track to spiritual stardom, or their chance to fame. While addressing a group of prospective ministers, the famous British pastor Charles Spurgeon[56] addressed this misguided view: "The pulpit is never to be the ladder by which ambition is to climb."[57] Genuine ministry is not a platform, but a service to humanity.

Others pursue ministry as a safe alternative. So many callings can be scary or feel overwhelming whether it is a call to politics, arts, business, or entertainment. These industries are often intimidating and require endurance to succeed.

I have had countless conversations with people who were giving up on the marketplace because their jobs were too tough or they felt their only way to succeed for the Lord was to go "full-time." Not long ago, a man was faltering at his business and felt it was his sign to go full-time. Instead of sharing here what I told him, I'll let Spurgeon speak to this notion:

"I have met ten, twenty, a hundred brethren, who have pleaded that they were sure, quite sure that they were called to the ministry . . . because they failed in everything else."[58] He goes on to say what I am convinced of, that those called to full-time ministry should be able to excel at most everything. In his words, "Jesus Christ deserves the best men to preach His cross, and not the empty-headed and the shiftless."[59]

Albeit harsh, but we get the point: in the end, the goal is to find your place on the team and become the best team member you can possibly be. The mission of the team is the same for everyone, whether it is in the marketplace

---

[56] I'll tell all about this great hero of the faith in the next chapter.
[57] Spurgeon, Charles. Lectures to My Students. Grand Rapids, MI: Zondervan, 1979, 35.
[58] Ibid., 37.
[59] Ibid., 38.

or Christian ministry, live for the kingdom of God[60] through releasing blessings, winning people to Christ, and making disciples. Some of Jesus' last words were, "Go and make disciples of the nations," and He gave this command to all His followers, not just the full-time ministers.

All Christians are called to help fulfill the Great Commission. In addition to making disciples and bringing transformation, marketplace members often have a unique opportunity to develop resources for the work of God and the parts of the team in desperate need of financial support. This is a critical component of any team.

Considering the quarterback again, we realize that he only gets paid when the front office manages contracts, generates fan interest, and creates a base of financial support.

If everyone went into ministry, how would the bills get paid? Where would the budget come from? Who would provide Bibles? How could there be stable salaries and support?

It is the same reason why the Levites were just one of the twelve tribes. The other eleven tribes were called to bring support so that they could be free to serve the Lord in the temple. The responsibility for success belongs to the entire team. *Each part does its work.*

Some of my greatest moments of need as a minister are for financial support. It may be for training centers in China, a new campus outreach, a church plant or an orphanage that needs a new roof. Thirty-plus years into full-time ministry, the needs are greater than ever, just as the world's needs are greater than ever.

I am one part of the team, but I could never do it alone. It takes the entire team. Each part does its work. Fortunately, I do not recall anyone ever saying to me, "All that guy wants is our money." The truth is it is not about

---

[60] When you include Matthew's circumlocution, "the kingdom of Heaven," Jesus speaks about "the kingdom of God" in fifty-seven different passages in the Gospels. That's more than any other subject. The arrival of the kingdom of God was the first thing He preached (Mark 1:15). It was what His followers where sent out to preach (Luke 9:20). Jesus also said that we should seek it first (Matthew 6:33). When He taught the disciples to pray, He instructed them to pray that God's kingdom would come on Earth, as it is in Heaven (Matthew 6:10).

me, the money, or even the need. It is about the team and our mission, which is to honor God and live for His kingdom on earth. The congregations and leaders I serve know it is my joy to work together. I am just grateful to be on the team, and I know it pleases the Lord when each part does its work.

I will never forget the law student from a prominent university whom I met early in his Christian walk. He was so excited about his new faith in Christ that he wanted to quit law school and be a missionary in China. He wanted a new spot on the team. He was sincere and earnest, but frankly, misguided. He had a false sense of what the Lord was asking him to do.

I cannot tell you how many times this story has repeated itself. I never want to squelch zeal, enthusiasm, or joy. I want people to be excited about the mission and what God is doing. But at the same time, God wants people to obey and follow **His calling**, not to create a life of sacrifice that He does not require. I love what the prophet Samuel told Saul, ". . . obedience is better than sacrifice."[61]

If God calls you to be the next Steve Jobs, do not try to improve His calling by being the next Mother Teresa. Although both extraordinary individuals have passed on, the point remains, God knows what is best for you.

This process of sorting through and discovering your call is a critical moment in the life of every believer. My typical approach is to encourage someone to pray it through and carefully think about it from every angle. Take the time to get all the appropriate counsel. As Scripture says, "with many counselors they succeed."[62]

In the case of the brilliant young law student, I threw my regular approach of getting outside counsel out the window. I knew that, this time, I would have to personally challenge his reasoning.

I told him as strongly as I could not to go to China. I believed he had been created and molded with keen intelligence, clear gifts, and there was supernatural purpose in the years he invested in his law degree. Certainly, this was the conventional wisdom a parent would give, and pastors must speak up, too!

---

[61] 1 Samuel 15:22
[62] Proverbs 15:22

After a few days and intense prayer, he completely concurred. He thanked me for my honesty and has gone on to have amazing success in law, politics, and society. He is pursuing God's mission with passion and has never doubted his choice to stay in his profession. Having won major elections by landslide victories, he knows he is in a place set apart by God, specifically for him. Today, he is a celebrated believer in a very high political post. His assignment has brought much honor to God and a lot of victories for righteousness.

Not everyone needs to go into full-time ministry; everyone needs to find their spot on the team and fill it. *Each part does its work.*

In the next chapter, we will ask one key question everyone must answer before leaving their field of study, occupation, or job and going into full-time ministry.

This question has helped a lot of people make the right decision.

4
THE BIG QUESTION

"For when I preach the gospel, I cannot boast, since I am compelled to preach. woe to me if I do not preach the gospel! . . ."
1 Corinthians 9:16

Have you ever gone on a roller-coaster that was scary enough you started to look for an exit door soon after getting in line? As you are zig-zagging your way through the endless waiting line, you look to see what the people who are coming back look like. You are also checking out the drops in the ride from way down below. Your stomach is churning. You ask yourself if you're sure you need to go through with this at all.

Then, over in the corner, painted to blend in with the wall, you spot it. Sometimes, they call it "the escape door."

It is an exit, usually disguised to minimize embarrassment. At the big theme parks, they are conveniently located at strategic spots before you reach the point of no return. Those in charge want you to know you do not have to get on the ride if you are having second thoughts.

Before we go any further here, I must ask you an "escape door" question. It is a BIG question. It is a "line-in-the-sand, difficult, scary, gut-check, defining moment" kind of question. Really, it is a question that God may be asking you as you pray through this decision to give your life to full-time ministry: **Are you able to do anything else and be fulfilled?**

The question is not, *"Can* you do something else?" I am sure you have plenty of skills or gifts that you could make a career out of, or at least earn a living.

The question is not, "Are you *willing* to do this?" Being willing is not the same as having a passion. I doubt that as you have dreamed of finding that perfect someone, your greatest desire was to find a spouse who was willing. No, what you want in a life partner is passion. You hope this special someone will do anything to be with you, that there is no other place they would rather be. God is the same way.

There was a young man in London who responded with this kind of passion to the call of God; he declared there was nothing he would rather do with his life than preach the gospel. Like Paul, he was compelled. He would rather die than not preach. At age nineteen, he took the pastorate of the largest Baptist church in the area, one that had begun to dwindle and decline. He preached the Word with power, and, as he did, the Spirit of God began to fill that place. Thousands came from all around to hear him preach, and were forever changed.

Without the use of audio amplification, he would regularly preach to crowds of more than 10,000. By age twenty-two, he was the most renowned preacher of his era, and to this day he is referred to as, "the Prince of Preachers." In time, he started a seminary to teach and train young ministers. Now known as Spurgeon's College, it is still training hundreds for missions and ministry today.[63]

Many of the lectures to his students were collected and published. I mentioned and cited him briefly in the last chapter, his name is Charles Spurgeon,[64] but his thoughts on this matter deserve a much closer look. I have read, re-read, and referred to Lectures to My Students on countless occasions. He has a lot to say on this issue of ministry as a vocation and was not afraid to challenge his pupils. Here is one great example, "Do not enter the ministry if you can help it . . . If any student in this room could be content to be a newspaper editor, or a grocer, or a farmer, or a doctor, or a lawyer, or a senator, or a king, in the name of heaven and earth let him go his way."[65]

Spurgeon's purpose here is not to diminish the contribution of certain professions. If that were the case, he would not have been a pillar in his community, serving and loving grocers, farmers, editors, lawyers, doctors,

---

[63] For more information, check out their website at www.spurgeons.ac.uk/.

[64] Spurgeon lived from 1834 – 1892 and preached more than 3,600 sermons in his lifetime. He published roughly
49 volumes during his lifetime and dozens more have been compiled since.

[65] Spurgeon, Charles. Lectures to My Students. Grand Rapids, MI: Zondervan, 1979, 26-27.

and newspaper editors. Rather, he is trying to clarify. Out of his love for his students, he wants to ensure they realize what they are in for.

I am sure that, from time to time, some of the students in his program were enamored with Spurgeon and his success. That is not all bad. All Christians, especially ministers, should lead lives that others will want to follow and emulate. But there is a big difference between wanting to be like someone you admire and passionately pursuing the call of God, yourself.

That pursuit is something God has made each one of us for, whether or not the pursuit leads us to full-time ministry. Our work should be an act of worship. It is a sacred activity—not secular—no matter what our job may be. God wants to give us that kind of passion for whatever we do, but, because the realities of life in ministry are often so different from our perceptions, it is critical that the prospective minister is committed and passionate, no matter what transpires in his life.

Not because he is drawn to the lifestyle. Not because he thinks it might be fun. Not because it might be an opportunity to be closer to God. There needs to be a compelling sense that "I must do this." Spurgeon continues, "We must feel that woe unto us if we preach not the gospel; the Word of God must be unto us as fire in our bones, otherwise, if we undertake the ministry, we shall be unhappy in it, shall be unable to bear the self-denials incident to it, and shall be of little service to those among whom we minister."[66] He was quite strong on this point when he said,"I have such a profound respect for this 'fire in the bones,' that if I did not feel it myself, I must leave the ministry at once."[67]

Judging what it is like to be a full-time minister by what you see on Sunday or Wednesday night will not provide a full view. What people see in meetings is such a small part of what this life of ministry entails. The overwhelming majority of ministry does not happen in the limelight; it does not cater to your pride or ego. It is often thankless,[68] and very few make it to the public renown of Judah Smith, Luis Palau, or Joyce Meyer. It is a calling of service to Christ. It requires sacrifice.

---

[66] Ibid., 27.

[67] Ibid., 28.

[68] In Luke 17:12-17, Jesus heals ten men of leprosy, and only one returns to say, "Thank you."

The late professor and theologian Edmund Clowney put it best, "Advancement in the kingdom is not by climbing but by kneeling. Since the Lord has become Servant of all, any special calling in his name must be a calling to humility, to service. The stairway to the ministry is not a grand staircase but a back stairwell that leads down to the servants' quarters"[69]

If it is not done out of the right motives, you will probably give up quickly. At some point along the way ministry produces an intense desire. I would describe this desire as virtually irresistible. Sooner or later, this call must be something that you own, that you steward out of obedience. The turnover rate is already too high.

In the pastorate alone, more than 1,700 ministers resign each month[70] due to moral failure, burnout, or contention with their local churches. This number does not include turnover among missionaries and people in full-time roles outside of pastor. This staggering number shows the call must be pursued with wisdom, diligence, and a sober understanding of the cost and challenge it holds in store.

The purpose of mentioning these statistics is not to invalidate or condemn those who have been released for ministry or called back to the marketplace. I have seen instances where those starting in full-time ministry later discover it is not their long-term calling and move on to further success in the marketplace. This is honorable.

Ministry is not a way to fame and fortune, and it is not the kind of profession that carries with it widespread popularity, although that may happen. There have been many young prospective ministers who have broken the news to Mom and Dad, only to be ridiculed or scolded for not pursuing a more "respectable" career.

When God calls you and it becomes your passion, you must respond regardless of the cost. Over the years, I have known numerous students from respected, world-class universities, like Duke and Columbia, who have answered the call to full-time ministry, despite their prestigious academic

---

[69] Clowney, Edmund. Called to the Ministry. Phillipsburg, New Jersey: Presbyterian and Reformed Publishing Co., 1964, 9.

[70] Expastors.com/why-do-so-man-pastors-leave-the-ministry-the-facts-will-shock-you

training and scholastic achievements. You can imagine this choice does not always go over too well with parents who invested so much into their education and are counting on prosperous returns.

As a parent, I can certainly understand how this feels. Yet I also realize that when a young person answers the call of God and is used to accomplish His mission and advance His kingdom, God's blessings flow to the entire family.

It may not initially look the way they thought it would, and it will not likely come on their timeframe, but, make no mistake, it will come. In my second year of full-time ministry, my secular, mystic, and artistic father came to visit me to learn more about my life and profession. By the end of the week, he cried out to Jesus for salvation, and I baptized him in my apartment. As a result, he and many others began to follow Jesus as well. As we answer the call, we are available to reach people whom we would have thought impossible.

When you answer the call of God in faith, He will meet your needs—from financial to emotional, spiritual to relational—to accomplish His will. He promises this in His Word, and I know from experience, He is faithful. Spurgeon describes the simplicity and seriousness of this process:

> This desire must be a thoughtful one. It should not be a sudden impulse unattended by anxious consideration. It should be the outgrowth of our heart in its best moments, the object of our reverent aspirations, the subject of our most fervent prayers. It must continue with us when tempting offers of wealth and comfort come into conflict with it, and remain as a calm, clear-headed resolve after everything has been estimated at its right figure, and the cost rightly counted.[71]

There is a big difference between being called to ministry and making an emotional decision. This is not to say that the call of God is not emotional; what I mean is it is not uncommon for people to get the feeling they should go into ministry, only to have that feeling wane. The call of God endures over time. In fact, it grows stronger until you feel you can no longer resist.

---

[71] Spurgeon, Charles. Lectures to My Students. Grand Rapids, MI: Zondervan, 1979, 28.

For many, this calling is described more as a process than a one-time, indescribable moment, like Isaiah experienced in Isaiah 6:6-8.

That is why I suggest you take the time you need to really pray through this. Sometimes, God calls people quickly, but, most of the time, this process of praying through and discovering your call, getting input and counsel from those you look to and trust takes time.

Processing the call alone in prayer is not sufficient. One cannot discern the call without pastors, seasoned mentors, and leadership input. Many well-intentioned people try to go out and "change the world" on their own. It seems to be a mantra of every group. While well-intentioned, it is misguided. The process involves leaders you trust even when they tell you what you do not want to hear. Their involvement may be possibly the most significant voice in your entire process.

Even as I am writing this, a 33-year-old successful, midtown Manhattan lawyer announced to me he was considering God's call to the full-time ministry. I immediately pushed back with all the reasons he should reconsider. He is skilled at his craft, working his way up through the ranks. He is realizing his dreams. Surely, God can use him right where he is. As we talked, he would not be deterred. His burning bush was burning too strong. His call to pursue ministry full-time simply will not be put out or extinguished.

Bottom line: He is no longer able to do anything else and be fulfilled. In the end of the process, God answered his call while maintaining his profession. This man helped start a new church on the upper east side of Manhattan, has become an elder, and continues to provide extraordinary teaching and leadership while maintaining a legal career.

Over time, this passion leads us to a make a clear decision. Most often, it is a process. Make no mistake, the choice is very personally yours. For me, it was a choice that, ultimately, I had to make. God does not force us. He will not make you do this against your will. He will not trick you into it. He is looking for the man or the woman who comes with a willing, passionate heart. As Isaiah eagerly responded, "Here I am. Send me!"[72]

---

[72] Isaiah 6:8 (NASB)

A friend of mine went to college to become a sports journalist. He went to a prestigious university that had a world-class journalism department and was quickly given tremendous opportunities to excel in his field. At the same time, he became a part of a thriving campus ministry at his school. He was continuing to grow in his faith and his involvement with the ministry. By the end of his sophomore year, he had a strong feeling God was calling him into the ministry. In his heart, he agreed he would obey this call and go wherever God would send him, though he continued in his studies and involvement with journalism.

One year later at the end of his junior year, he was offered his dream job in journalism. He would get to cover the NFL for a major network with a staggering initial salary. His prospective employer said it was not even necessary to finish his last year at the university. As he told me this story, he said that in that moment he realized this offer was God's way of showing him He would not force him to follow the call to ministry. Instead, he had the privilege of choosing full-time ministry, so, as he considered both options, he concluded that ministry was a good choice. It was not just good, it was amazing.

Like Paul, my friend was compelled. As Spurgeon had recommended, his decision was a thoughtful one, it was not impulsive, and, so, it compelled him, even when offers of wealth and comfort came into conflict.

My friend turned down the journalism offer and answered God's call to ministry. Eventually, he returned to lead a campus chapter at the same school he attended and saw many students lives transformed with the gospel. There were seasons of lack, trials, and all forms of adversity, but he has never regretted the choice he made.

What about you? Is there a job offer out there that would be more compelling than the call to preach the gospel full-time? Has your response to this call been thoughtful or impulsive? How would you respond to offers of wealth and comfort that would conflict with the call to full-time ministry? Let me reiterate: it is a BIG question.

It can be daunting to come up with an answer. It may put a lot of pressure on you, but there are ways you can figure out just how to respond. Perhaps you should go on a short-term mission trip. There is nothing like giving your full-time attention to the work of the ministry, even for a short time. It is a great way to measure and consider your call. You could also spend the next season volunteering to assist or serve your ministry director, pastor, campus pastor, or a missionary. This will give you better insight and access to what their day-to-day life is like, and provide you with a practical perspective on what the life of ministry is going to be.

A larger commitment might be participating in a ministry internship program. This is another great way to test your call, to see if you have the desire, the gifts, and the grace. It can be one more way for God to confirm your desire for service. Do not be shy about "experimenting" before jumping in full-time. The more thoughtful and thorough you are, the more certain and confident you will be.

Now that we understand the big question and how to arrive at potential answers, in the next chapter we will explore where to go next, and why it is so critical to start small.

Aletheia internship?
Volunteering for campus ministry w/ Kevin?
I've never really ministered to guys before...
Maybe Martin?
Scott ish?

5

START SMALL

"Whoever can be trusted with very little, can also be trusted with much, and whoever is dishonest with very little, will also be dishonest with much."
Jesus[73]

We have grown up in a world of instant gratification. Too often, "right now" is not soon enough. If you are like me, you can even find yourself getting impatient waiting three minutes for the microwave to finish your popcorn!

We have all had these experiences. We pick up a golf club and, in one lesson, expect to be a PGA golfer. We get a new guitar and write a song, and we dream of our song topping the charts. Anyone reading this book knows that there is no shortcut to success. Going into the ministry is no different.

When Jesus talked about starting, He always talked about the value of starting small. Most importantly, He set the example; with just twelve initial followers, Jesus turned the world upside down. Beginning with just 12, there are now more than 2.4 billion followers of Jesus world-wide·[74]

Often, Jesus' most quoted illustrations involved seeds. It is difficult to find anything smaller to the human eye than a seed. When Jesus talks about seeds, it is always in the context of sowing something small, trusting in faith that eventually it will become significant.[75]

If you have ever planted anything, you know that "eventually" is not instant. You do not microwave seeds. All the Miracle Grow in the world

---

[73] Luke 16:10

[74] "Christianity 2015: Religious Diversity and Personal Contact" (PDF). gordonconwell.edu. January 2015. Retrieved 2016-10-28.

[75] There are several passages to choose from (especially in Matthew), but your starting point should be "the Parable of the Sower," one Jesus' cornerstone teachings. You can find alternate versions in Mark 4, Matthew 13, and Luke 8.

will not make "eventually" become instantaneous. How long does it take for a seed to grow into a tree? It takes years. At first, the tree does not look too impressive. It does not usually grow straight. There are weird branches sprouting in different directions. Some years, it may not look like the tree is growing at all. Yet, in other years, when the conditions are just right, it will grow at an accelerated rate.

I have found that ministry so often grows likes seeds and trees. When it starts, it is diminutive. I mean as small as "how-could-anything-happen-from-this" small. Ministry typically takes a long time to grow, and it often does not look impressive on the way.

This has certainly been my story of Christian ministry. Not long after I answered the call, I launched a new church and was hanging on to one verse that framed everything: "And though your beginning was small, your latter days will be very great." (Job 8:7 ESV) Over the years, this ministry has multiplied into fifteen nations and thousands of disciples made for Christ.

Even more dramatically, in 1984, Rice Broocks and Steve Murrell started at church in the heart of university belt of metro Manila, Philippines, a politically turbulent city. What started out small in Manila is now a movement of multiple churches ... reaching more than 100,000 people in 30 years.

Fortunately, with perseverance and diligent care over time, ministry grows into something great and significant. Significance may not be measured in numbers, but in obedience toward God and the transformation of individual lives.

There is a clear principle here that Jesus describes in the quote that starts this chapter: "whoever can be trusted with little, eventually can be trusted with much, but the one who is dishonest or untrustworthy with a little should not be trusted with a lot."[76]

What does this mean for ministry? If there is a job opening in ministry, one that features large beautiful facilities, thousands of people, and a massive

---

[76] Luke 16:10

budget, you will get a sea of applications. It is not hard to feel called under those circumstances.

However, if you find an opening that requires long hours for little pay, meets in coffee shops and dorm rooms with disinterested students who cuss you out on your first day, you will not get the same widespread, eager response.

Very few of us like to start small, but, most of the time, God insists that we do.

He never seems to be in a hurry. In fact, He seems to be as concerned with the process of growth and what happens during the long, slow grind as He is with the finished product. The process is of great value and importance to God.

It never ceases to amaze me when I hear someone's story about the great things God has done in their life, almost always, things started so small. When I was in the Middle East meeting with Jews, Arabs, and Muslims, I met a middle-aged woman, named Karen. Years ago, she lived with her teenage son in a refugee camp in Palestinian Jericho, struggling for clean drinking water and killing scorpions. In a time when many experts believed it was impossible to go and preach the gospel in that part of the world, Karen went to serve through basic humanitarian efforts. Five years after she founded her church, she has more than 300 Muslim believers[77] worshipping Jesus. This is quite a feat for a single mom who was serving as a humanitarian.

Rick Warren, Craig Groeschel, Tony Evans, and a host of others did not grow their churches or ministries to incredible size overnight. Many have built upon the seeds God led their spiritual fathers to sow, and, today, they reap the harvest. In truth, all of us build upon the work of others who have invested time, prayers and resources before us.

---

[77]Many of these are members of Hamas and Fatah, military Muslim political parties that are considered terrorist organizations.

Here are several examples of areas where God consistently asks us to start small:

1. FRUIT

"Fruit" is biblical language for "results." The world of the Bible is a pre-modern, agricultural world. In that world, fruit or harvest is what the growing season produced. "Fruit" in ministry terms can be understood as the result of a season of ministry.

These results can be both quantitative and qualitative. It can be the number of people who hear the gospel, as well as the measure of spiritual transformation in the life of a believer. It can be how many people give their lives to Christ and the depth of relationships that are developed in the community. Or it can be the number of people added to your ministry, church, or fellowship.

Often, the tendency in the early days of ministry is to expect instant and massive fruit; we think we should see hundreds respond to the gospel in a short amount of time. We expect to produce the highest quality messages and give world-class wisdom and counsel to all. Too often, we view anything less as failure.[78] I truly hope that happens with you, but with most of us, it is nothing like that.

Earlier, I mentioned my first day of full-time ministry. In those days, having twenty people in a room was like an ocean of humanity. There were times when nobody showed up and an evangelistic Bible study was instantly turned into my personal quiet time. And because I felt defeated, they were very "quiet" times.

Going back to Jesus' principle of demonstrating our trustworthiness in the little things reminded me that a harvest of exemplary fruit is always preceded by consistent, progressive growth.

The patient and passionate communication of the gospel that results in a single transformed life is the starting place for a dynamic ministry of

---

[78] After all, Peter had 3,000 respond the first time he preached. You can read this story for yourself in Acts 2.

evangelism. As James said, "Be patient, therefore, brothers, until the coming of the Lord. See how the farmer waits for the precious fruit of the earth, being patient about it, until it receives the early and the late rains. You also, be patient. Establish your hearts for the coming of the Lord is at hand." (James 5:7-8)

The disciplined and faithful management of a small group needs to take place before a minister is given the responsibility of shepherding a congregation. That is why all fruit is so significant; not only should we celebrate the excitement and joy of the current results, but we should anticipate each sign of success as an indicator of bigger things yet to come.

If you feel God is calling you to full-time ministry, one of the greatest ways you can respond in obedience is to give all your passion and energy to the small responsibilities you have now. Do not see them as insignificant, but view them as opportunities to demonstrate your trustworthiness, knowing that, in time, God will trust you with more.

don't see very much fruit → *question it*

Where is the fruit in your life? What is it communicating to you about your calling? Are you showing yourself to be trustworthy in the small things? Are you watching over your time? Are you faithfully giving and budgeting your finances?

The presence of genuine fruit in a person's life goes a long way in establishing credibility. When a young person chooses not to pursue a career path requiring several years of school, parents are often puzzled or upset. If, however, you can point to the fruit of lives that are being changed, people who are being transformed, and the tangible blessings that the ministry of their son or daughter is accomplishing, it becomes hard to argue against such a call.

In contrast, if there is only a feeling, only the potential for calling without any of the smallest signs of fruit, it is probably time to question this call. This is why I recommend short-term missions, local involvement, and internships as great opportunities to evaluate a potential minister's call.

If you are not seeing fruit in your area of ministry, it does not necessarily mean that you are not called. Perhaps, you should be re-evaluated and given a different assignment more in-line with your gifting and calling.

2. FINANCES

Few things in life create pressure like financial need. The ability to endure and overcome in the face of great financial need is an integral part of responding in obedience to the call to full-time ministry.

Again, following Jesus' principle, we should be willing to start small. The amount of pressure and responsibility of managing the budget of a thousand-member church is a lot more difficult than raising enough money to go on a short-term mission trip. Obeying God and trusting Him for funds to go on that trip is a great first step towards being entrusted with the budget of a larger ministry.

Starting small allows us to demonstrate discipline and responsibility that become the building blocks upon which we can grow. As a single person, tithing, giving offerings, living within your means, and balancing your budget requires less faith and discipline than when you are married or have a family. When you are faithful to consistently meet the mark, you demonstrate a trustworthiness that allows God to give you more responsibility and opportunity in days to come.

When I first started in ministry, I did not have much, and the needs seemed impossible to meet. Many years later, if I had known then what my financial challenges would look like today and what God would ask me to believe for, I probably would have passed out or put in for early retirement!

People may look at the facilities and various outreaches I oversee now—those that have cost millions of dollars to launch and sustain—and be quick to pass judgment on how easily we got here. We must all be careful in our criticism of someone's apparent success or prosperity. I can still vividly recall times when I had no food wondering how God would ever provide enough when the weekly offering was barely $200.

When I first started in ministry, I hardly had a salary. Sure, I had a vision, but you cannot eat vision. We were working with students, and I remember one particular instance when my family literally ran out of food. If I, alone, had to rough it, that would have been one thing, but I had a family to provide for, and they were all hungry!

I prayed and asked God to provide and felt like He simply said, "Consider it pure joy when you face various kinds of trials."[79] So in faith, I chose gratitude and happiness despite my lack. Trust me, when you look in your fridge and all you see is a stick of butter and an old can of spaghetti sauce, it is a choice to rejoice.

Out of the blue, on that same day, a neighbor girl delivered a giant crate of oranges I had completely forgotten I had purchased earlier in the year to support her school project. In that moment, oranges were, to us, like manna[80] had been to the Israelites.

We had orange juice for breakfast, orange slices for lunch, and orange soufflé for dinner! Okay, not really, but we sure did get creative dreaming up different ways to eat oranges. Through that provision, God didn't let us go hungry. I will never forget that miracle of provision. He answered my prayer and provided for us, just like He promised.

By God's grace and blessings, our ministry in North Carolina has given away far more than $10 million to charity and missions to date. For some, such as Warren Buffett, this is not much at all, but, for a ministry that started with $200 a week, it is not a bad beginning!

The temptations we face at this stage can be great as well. Sadly, there are too many stories of those in full-time ministry whose character has let them and their supporters down. The enemy does not wait until the stakes are high to tempt us; he tempts us regularly, and when he finds an area where we are vulnerable, he attacks us whenever and wherever he can do the most damage.

That is why character and integrity with finances is so important. If you will build years of character and discipline in this area, you will have the faith and character to stand in the days when your obedience affects so many more than just yourself. If your financial status could be a stumbling block to yourself or others, you should assess and correct your finances before pursuing full-time ministry.

---

[79] He was pointing me to James 1:2 in His Word.

[80] In Exodus, God feeds the starving people of Israel in the desert every day with supernatural food called manna that appeared on the ground for them every morning. Our supernatural provision didn't appear on the ground, it arrived in a crate!

3. RECOGNITION AND PROMOTION

We live in a celebrity culture. Many would rather be infamous than anonymous. People want to stand out and be recognized, to make a name for themselves, to somehow achieve their fifteen minutes of fame. Sadly, the church is often not much different. Just as there are celebrities in entertainment, athletics, and politics, there are also celebrities in ministry.
I believe God promotes people, and the Bible tells us in Proverbs that a person who is skilled at what they do will not stay in obscurity but will serve kings.[81] Proverbs also tells us that our reputation, what we are known for, is more valuable than riches.[82]

Perhaps more than in any other vocation, the full-time minister needs to be willing to start small. Before you concern yourself with how to become a household name, work on developing character and demonstrating Christ-like love so you can have a great name in your own home and community.

Most full-time ministers will fulfill their call without large-scale recognition. For every well-known minister, there are thousands of faithful men and women who serve without acclaim, without the general public's awareness, yet they make eternal contributions. Jesus described how the Father will evaluate and reward Kingdom contributions, saying, "But many who are first will be last, and many who are last will be first." Matthew 19:30

At the end of the day, it is all about our faithfulness to God: Did we do what He asked? Were we faithful stewards of the talents He gave us? If so, our grand entrance to heaven will be greeted with the words we all long to hear: "Well done, my good and faithful servant . . . Enter into the joy of your master."[83]

Lifting up your name or the name of your ministry is not the goal; the goal is to lift up the name of Jesus and His kingdom, so that His great name can be famous and honored throughout the whole earth. In short, "It's for the fame of His Name!"

If you focus on building a reputation of character, integrity, kindness as a

---

[81] Proverbs 22:29
[82] Proverbs 22:1
[83] Matthew 25:23

young minister, and you show Christ-like love with those in your apartment building or on your street, God will take care of promoting you. If you honor Jesus, the true Star, if you make His story most important, your leadership will take people to the true Source that never stumbles, the Great Shepherd who cares for souls. Having done this, your true satisfaction and joy will remain.

By building your ministry this way, if and when God does bring you larger recognition, it will be the kind that honors Him and propels your ministry and calling into greater fruitfulness. If it does not happen—if you remain "hidden" to the masses—you will not feel any loss nor miss out on the joy that comes from making the name of Jesus great.

The longer you hesitate to build in this way, the more difficult it becomes. That is why it is so critical that you start from day one, when things are small. Small seeds faithfully tended, bear much fruit that lasts, building character that also lasts.

4. RESOURCES

You may not think of yourself as an administrator or manager, but if you respond to this call to full-time ministry, you cannot escape it. There is an unavoidable component of managing and administrating resources that always goes with ministry. When you first start, those resources may simply be your time, a small amount of financial support, and possibly a few volunteers.

Management is both a skill and a gift. This means people are gifted with different levels of ability, but as a skill all of us can improve. Various roles and positions in ministry will carry varying levels of management and administrative resources. This is why it is important for you to start small.

Jesus demonstrates this principle in the parable of the talents.[84] In the story, a talent is the name for a sum of money, roughly equivalent to twenty years of a day-laborer's wage.[85] In the parable a wealthy businessman leaves on

---

[84] Matthew 25:14-30
[85] From the TNIV footnotes, p.915

a journey and gives five talents to one servant, two to another, and one to another, "each according to his ability."[86] They were all given the chance to manage and administrate resources, but they were not given equal amounts because they did not have the same ability.

When the businessman returns, both the servant with five talents and the one with two used the resources and doubled their money. The last servant, out of fear of his boss, hid the money and only gave him back what he had been given. So the businessman took that one talent and gave it to the one who had ten.

As you bear responsibility for your resources, you will not have the time to be concerned about what God has given you compared to others. Instead, you are to concentrate on how you are showing yourself trustworthy and faithful with the resources you have. You are not responsible for something you do not have. From the parable and in so many life situations, we see the driving principle behind starting small: faithful in little, faithful in much.[87]

In your early days of ministry, it is not wise to accept more resources than you can handle. Learn the value of strategically turning down opportunities because they will keep you from being faithful with the ones you already have.

When I was young, I made the common mistake of saying yes to everything. I wish I would have known better. Today, I still get overcommitted and continue to need help in this area, but I am getting better, and, now, I certainly know better. Willingly start small with your resources, knowing that, as you show yourself faithful and trustworthy, you will be ready to accept greater responsibility when God brings it.

What should you do if you are already in over your head? What if in trying to produce massive and instantaneous fruit, your marriage and family are suffering?

What if you did not start small with your finances and you have begun to fall behind and into debt?

---

[86] Matthew 25:15
[87] This is the principle of Luke 16:10

There are three kinds of people in the world: the "haves," the "have-nots," and the "have-not-paid-for-what-they-have." If you are in this third category in a serious way (saddled with exorbitant loans beyond a college education or an appreciating item, such as a home), you may have to deal with this before considering full-time ministry. When you have an extreme amount of debt, it becomes difficult to keep your focus off your finances and on your ministry.

It could be that full-time ministry is not the best fit for you. It could also be that it is a right fit, but now is not the right time. This is why God's lack of separation between sacred and secular work is so brilliant. Sometimes, it is better to serve in the marketplace without compromising your future call to full-time ministry.

People often are tempted to feel embarrassed because their road does not look ideal in their mind, or is not like someone else's. Let me encourage you today. God can move you around from one kind of work to another to fulfill the calling He has given you. He is always loving, always patient and kind, and always working in us to accomplish His purpose.

So, there it is. With your fruit, your finances, your recognition/promotion, and your resources, don't be afraid to start small. Do not be discouraged with where God has you. Act like the future of the world hinges on your character because, in reality, it does! As you are obedient and faithful with what God has entrusted to you, He will bring increase in each of these areas.

Let us start small and be faithful, trusting that, in time, God will cause us to grow and succeed even beyond our wildest dreams.

6
PREPARATION
AND TRAINING

*"Do your best to present yourself to god as one approved, a worker
who does not need to be ashamed and who correctly handles the
word of truth. . ."*
2 Timothy 2:15

Reverend John Harvard founded Harvard College in 1636 for one reason: **to
train clergymen to be prepared for the ministry.**

Here is an excerpt from the "rules and principles" (something like a student
handbook) in 1642: "Let every student be plainly instructed, and earnestly
pressed to consider well, the main end of his life and studies is, to know God
and Jesus Christ which is eternal life ..." This quote was to be the spiritual
foundation for the education and calling of a young minister at Harvard
College. In addition, a proficiency in Latin and Greek was required for
admission. The educational component was a seriously rigorous academic
ordeal.[88]

Methods of preparation have changed since the founding of Harvard
and down through the 2,000-year history of the church. For a long time,
prospective ministers embraced a monastic lifestyle and went off for years
to quietly pray and study the Scriptures along with church tradition. Many
times, they never came back to the world, but the sole pursuit of their lives
became a life of prayer and study.

For the past hundred years or so, the dominant vehicle for ministry training
has been denominational seminaries. If a young person wants to become a
pastor or a missionary, they typically find a seminary affiliated with their

---

[88] 106 of the first 108 universities or colleges in the United States were started by a church or
Christians. At one point, Jonathan Edwards, a giant among American pastors and leaders in
history, served as the president of Princeton.

denomination. Seminaries offer graduate degrees in a variety of ministry-specific roles and fields. Once you complete your study, you apply to various job openings overseen by the denomination. Because this is the traditional model of training, there is often an expectation that going into the ministry means enrolling in a seminary. For many, this may be a great way to start. For others, like me, it is increasingly common that seminary and academic pursuits come long after early years of ministry and build on top of practical ministry experience.

Although training and education are essential, one of the clearest things we have learned through church history is this: character, leadership skills, and anointing from God are far more important than a graduate degree. God's calling is not validated by just acquiring a degree, but it is confirmed by a demonstration of the necessary gifts, Christ-like character, and consistent, lasting fruit.

At the same time, training and ongoing development are essential for all full-time ministers. Without a doubt, ill-equipped ministers are ineffective and incapable of meeting the challenges and demands this calling brings and our culture demands.

Therefore, the question most important to ask is, "What kind of training or education will help me most effectively obey God and complete His call at this stage in my life?" Approaching training from this perspective allows for flexibility for different people and different callings, during a variety of seasons. For example, it is becoming more and more common for pastors and leaders to combine in-house training with practical hands-on experience before adding seminary training to the mix.

Many organizations are recognizing this intermediate step and are developing Bible/ministry schools and training programs designed either as a part of the overall discipleship process for all believers or as an introductory program for full-time ministers just beginning in the church or organization. These programs have tremendous value as a starting place to develop a basic working knowledge that can be built upon during a ministry career as needs and opportunities arise.

For this approach to work, we must demonstrate the attitude found in 2

Timothy 2:15. Each of us must keep doing our best to present ourselves to God as a worker who is unashamed because we have ~~correctly understood~~ handled the Word of God.

Doing our best means we are always growing, learning, and willing to work hard to improve our skills. Skillful evangelism, apologetics, a good understanding of the Bible, Christian theology (theology proper, anthropology, Christology, and soteriology), and basic people skills are the building blocks for becoming a strong minister.[89] Many of these skills can be acquired through academic courses or local church programs.

Secondly, we are presenting ourselves to God. It is His approval—and not man's— that we are after. Out of our love and reverence for Him, we work as hard as we can to represent Him in a way that brings honor to His name. In this sense, our devotion and devotional life is more important than our degrees.

As the apostle Paul said in 2 Timothy 2:15, we do not want to be ashamed. In ministry, we will be faced with the difficult task of articulating unpopular ideas and controversial concepts in a post-Christian secular society. If we have done the hard work, though, we can make difficult truth acceptable with wisdom and skill.

I cannot tell you how many times I have cringed watching news anchors fire the same difficult question to fellow ministers: "Are you telling me that if I don't believe in Jesus, I'm going to hell?" Some are articulate and capable of responding, while others struggle to be coherent or convincing in explaining Christ as the only way to salvation.[90] If someone leaned in and fired that question at you with an audience of a million people watching, what would you say? Tough moments like this show the critical importance of training. Opportunities always come to those who are best prepared.

Finally, we need to correctly handle the words of truth. How we communicate is often as important as what we communicate. To correctly handle the

---

[89] Definitions as follows: theology proper – study of God; anthropology – study of man and sin; Christology – study of Jesus; soteriology – study of salvation.
[90] John 14:6

words of truth means we not only maintain truth, but we speak the truth in love, rather than recklessly cutting people with our words.[91]

There are few things worse than a poorly dressed preacher whose veins are popping out of his neck while he is getting visibly distraught in a public interview. The Bible is so clear that our words are to be "seasoned with grace"[92] and our demeanor is to be Christ-like.[93] When our words and attitudes match these standards, our ministry will be persuasive and effective.[94]

FOUR AREAS OF TRAINING

I find it helpful to think about education and training in four different areas: Bible and theology, leadership, practical ministry skills, and culture and contemporary issues.

1. BIBLE AND THEOLOGY

Every full-time minister needs to have a solid understanding of the Bible—how to read, understand, and apply it to daily life. They must also have the capacity to communicate and articulate biblical truth effectively. This ability should always be growing. Though this seems obvious and hardly worth mentioning, unfortunately, it must be stated emphatically.

An intern or first-year minister needs to have at least a basic overview of Scripture as a whole. He must understand its major themes, have an understanding of the Old and New Testaments, possess a clear and healthy knowledge of Jesus and His role in God's plan, and have a concise and accurate view of the gospel.

Do not let the word "theology" intimidate you! You may not think of yourself

---

[91] Proverbs 12:18

[92] Colossians 4:6

[93] Philippians 2:5

[94] Proverbs 15:1, 2 Peter 3:15, and Acts 26:28 give us insights to healthy communication. In Acts 26, Paul is on trial before the king, and, yet, he conducts himself in such a way that he ministers to the king and nearly persuades him to become a Christian. That is a great model of excellence for us to follow.

as a theologian, but if you have ideas about God, you have "theology" because the word simply means "the study of God." Make no mistake about it, you are a theologian. The issue is not whether you are one, but, rather, will you be a good one or bad one?

All ministers should have at least an introductory understanding of what the Bible says about the nature of God, the Trinity, the nature of man, the role and work of the Holy Spirit, Christology, soteriology, basic eschatology, and spiritual transformation. In addition, it is important they have at least a basic grasp of the historic Christian faith and how the body of Christ has wrestled through these issues up to now.

All believers, especially full-time ministers, should spend their lives studying and growing. As your unique calling develops, your responsibilities increase and the demands on your gifting and abilities are stretched. As this happens, you will need target areas of training and development.

I have often been asked questions for which I did not have an answer. Early on, I began the habit of writing down the question and the person's phone number, so I could take the question home to work on an adequate answer. I have found that people love this, because it shows sincerity and transparency. Full-time ministers need to be secure to say, "I love your question, but I need to think about it before I can answer. Would you be willing to talk about this more after I've had some time to pray and study?"

You may find there is an area of study or a new role that requires formal training and a season of more intense focus. Several of my colleagues have gone on to pursue doctorates to become more effective in their unique areas of ministry.

If you are going to go from leading a campus Bible study to planting a church, you are probably going to need some type of training. If you are going to go from reaching international students to doing children's ministry, you are definitely going to need new training! Most likely, this training will come at a considerable cost to your resources (primarily your money and time), so it is not wise to make this commitment lightly. Wait until you realize through prayer and counsel, that this kind of training is necessary and will open the doors God is calling you to walk through.

Remember, training, itself, is not an endorsement for ministry or a right to a job. Training does not make the minister, rather, it better prepares the minister for his or her next step.

2. LEADERSHIP

There is a big difference between being an employee and being an employer. The level of training you need to lead a Bible study is different than what you need to run a ministry staff of fifty full-time employees, ranging from youth and associate pastors to secretaries, daycare directors, and facility managers.

No matter what our current role or assignment is, all of us need to develop our leadership abilities. We need to work on our discipline and character, our people skills, our ability to make wise decisions, our productivity and efficiency, and our skills in making everyone around us better.

Thanks to the work of leadership guru John C. Maxwell[95] and others, we have been shown that leadership is more than a gift or a birthright. Leadership is influence, and, fortunately, it can be learned. When we become better leaders, we will have plenty of ministry opportunities for the rest of our lives.

Leadership is like intelligence; it involves both nature and nurture. You are naturally born with a certain amount, but, through hard work and the right approach, you can nurture and develop whatever amount you were given.

You do not have to be the boss to develop leadership skills. Many bosses prove that point. They may be the boss, but they are definitely not a leader. Leaders inspire people to follow them. They build trust and effective teams. Leadership has value for all of us, as individuals, as Christians, as members of families and communities, and as members of all kinds of teams.

---

[95] John C. Maxwell is the founder of EQUIP, an organization that trains and develops leaders in every nation of the world. He has sold more than 25 million books, and, in 2014, he was identified as the #1 leader in business by the American Management Association® and the most influential leadership expert in the world by Business Insider and Inc. magazine.

I remember reading a leadership book by John C. Maxwell called, *The 360-Degree Leader*. The big idea of this book dispels the myth that you must be at the top of an organization to lead. You can lead from anywhere, whether you are stuck in the middle, or at "the bottom of the heap."

This idea is consistent with countless biblical stories. One of my favorites is the account of Joseph,[96] the son of Jacob and the great-grandson of Abraham. Joseph never stopped dreaming, praying, or leading, despite his negative circumstances. He was thrown into a pit and rejected by his brothers. He was unjustly imprisoned, yet he continued to succeed and be promoted anyway. His leadership abilities led him out of the prison and straight into national prominence.

Joseph may have started in the pit, but he ended up in the palace. This could be the story of your life, too. You will find grace to lead in many places where you were not even invited. Do not wait on the invitation. When you see a need, take the lead. If you lead with character, integrity, and excellence, before long, you will have the recognition, too.

One of the indisputable things Jesus explains about leadership in the parable of talents is that when you are a leader and you are faithful handling responsibility, you will be given even more.[97] When you are given new leadership and management responsibilities, you will need new training and development as well.

One of the great surprises from my tenure in Christian ministry has been how much of what I have to do ultimately comes down to leadership. Leadership is not theological training, apologetics, debate and rhetoric, or even communication skills.

Leadership skills are what I have had to use daily to rally people to live for a cause that is greater than themselves. For the sake of the vision, I ask people to do this with teams they often do not know, without a salary, and, many times, to pay in advance with their time and resources.

Fortunately, there are more leadership tools available today than ever before.

---

[96] You can find Joseph's story in Genesis chapters 37-50.
[97] Matthew 25:14-30

As the old saying goes, "Leaders are readers." Build your library. Start a leadership small group with some peers and a few mentors who are willing to work with you to grow and expand your skills. Before you know it, you will be given more leadership roles in a variety of places.

3. PRACTICAL MINISTRY SKILLS

Though full-time ministry is primarily a calling, it is also a vocation, a unique profession that carries with it specific skills that must be developed. James 3:1 speaks to aspiring church leaders, "Dear brothers and sisters, not many of you should become teachers in the church, for we who teach will be judged more strictly" (NLT).

There are some specific responsibilities in which full-time ministers should be trained and skilled to perform: learning detailed techniques for effective preaching, wise and compassionate counseling, how to lead people to Christ, and administering the sacraments, are just a few.

These skills require instruction, practice and evaluation.[98] When you combine a genuine call to ministry with an obedient response, and mix in the right kind of training and development, lives will be changed, and the kingdom of God will certainly advance.

Just like any other skill, no matter how long you have done it, working on the basics with a constant focus on improvement will always raise the quality of work. Of course, this requires effort and humility, but what cause could be more worthwhile than partnering with God in His mission on earth?

It never ceases to amaze me how complicated people's problems can be. When I first started in the ministry, it was all about changing the world. I did not know I would be changing diapers first. Not only was I changing diapers, I changed two different kinds: natural diapers and spiritual diapers.

After years of sitting down with people and listening to their life stories, you will have heard it all. You will even hear things you wish you had never heard or knew existed. In those moments, training is critical, because it

---

[98] Robert Coleman's classic book The Master Plan of Evangelism addresses the process of discipleship from selection to delegation to supervision.

does not tend to go too well when a person opens their shattered life, and you respond by saying, "They never told me what to do with somebody like you!"

There are a variety of gifts that emerge over time in the life of a full-time minister, gifts that are greatly benefited by additional coaching. These gifts are given by Christ to build up the people God and to make ministry more enjoyable for those He has called. Prophecy, intercessory prayer, healing, worship, and hospitality are all examples of these types of gifts.

Romans 12:6 states, "We have different gifts, according to the grace given to us,"[99] and, throughout the New Testament,[100] Scripture encourages and explains the role of these gifts. God gives these gifts to all followers of Christ for the common good of the body. Part of the process of growing in our relationship involves understanding and moving in the unique gifts God has given us.[101]

These gifts usually emerge in the context of regular ministry, and can carry with them a new assignment or a change of direction. God's Word tells us that we should ask God for the gifts necessary to carry out His tasks (1 Cor. 12:1; James 1:5; Luke 11:3).

The indispensable element that makes practical ministry work so well is an intangible one, often called the "anointing of God." Although Jesus was in preparation during His thirty years on earth, His ministry did not begin until the Holy Spirit fell on Him during His baptism in the Jordan River. From that point forward, Jesus went about doing good and healing people.[102]

When God calls a young man or woman, He always adds His anointing so that the work they accomplish is of God and not of them. This anointing often comes through association with those from whom they want to learn and emulate.

---

[99] 1 Corinthians 7:7 says each person has their own gift from God.

[100] All of 1 Corinthians 12 describes the role and function of spiritual gifts. Chapter 14:1 says that we should eagerly desire them, and 14:12 says that we should go after the gifts that build up the church. 1 Peter 4:10 says that we should use these gifts to serve others as an administration of God's grace

[101] The classic book written on the subject by C. Peter Wagner, Discover Your Spiritual Gifts. Ventura, CA: Regal Books, 2005.

[102] This is how Peter described Jesus' ministry to the people at Cornelius' house in Acts 10:38.

Elisha stayed with and served Elijah. Thus, he received a double-portion of his powerful anointing.[103] Likewise, Timothy was mentored by Paul and he later received an anointing to be an apostle.[104] Being mentored, pastored, and discipled can have an amazing benefit and can release a greater anointing. This is more than a one-time meeting with someone you admire: it is a relationship. One of my greatest privileges in ministry has been to have three or four trusted mentors and spiritual fathers.

Practical ministry skills, coupled with the anointing of God, are the keys to an effective ministry. Skills are acquired, but the anointing is cultivated and received through the Holy Spirit. Receiving the anointing comes from walking with God and availing yourself to Him. When we walk with Him, we earnestly desire Him and the spiritual gifts (1 Corinthians 12:1, 14:1), and He gladly makes them available to us.

4. CULTURE AND CONTEMPORARY ISSUES

When you get to the bottom of it, ministry is about people. It is about serving, loving, leading, and having relationships with people. If you are given the privilege to do this, you need to speak the language of people, understand what drives them, what scares them, what they enjoy, and what matters to them most. In other words, you need to know them and their culture. In our multicultural world, culture is constantly changing.

I love that line from *The Wizard of Oz,* "Toto, I have a feeling we're not in Kansas anymore," because it reminds me how much our world has changed. I grew up in an era of record players, eight-track cassettes as big as a brick, and a three-channel black-and-white TV with rabbit ears covered in tinfoil.

Our video game of choice was called *Pong.* Looking back, it was hilarious to think we could play *Pong* for hours. It was hooked up to the TV set and had a paddle that would hit a ball back and forth as it bounced off various lines. If you knew a little physics and had good hand-eye coordination, you could bounce that ball off the line for hours.

---

[103] 2 Kings 2:9

[104] In the opening verse of each of the letters to the church in Thessalonica, Timothy is included as an authority figure. When considering the manner Paul talked to Timothy in each of his letters, I read that inclusion to mean that Paul saw Timothy as an apostle, a significant authority figure in more than one church.

We thought it was cool, but *Pong* has not stood the test of time. Thanks to Sony, Microsoft, and Nintendo, things have dramatically changed. Fortunately, we serve and represent a God who makes Himself known in every culture. He engages people in their culture, right where they are, with His presence and His kingdom.

Jesus said that the greatest command is to love God and to love people.[105] If we are serious about doing this, we cannot stay in the safe walls of our churches and Christian communities. We must go boldly into the culture where people live.

The Bible is filled with examples of people who lived this way. We read of one of the tribes of Israel as "understanding the times and knowing what Israel should do."[106] The Lord gave Daniel and his friends the ability to understand all kinds of literature and learning as they lived in the immoral culture of Babylon.[107]

Paul preached to the crowds in Athens at Mars Hill using the work of their own philosophers and artists as his metaphors. This story found in Acts 17 is a great study on effective cross-cultural apologetics and evangelism. When Paul spoke in the familiar setting of the synagogue, he opened the scroll and spoke of Christ from the Torah (the Hebrew law that "marked them" as the people of God) and the prophets. When he went to pagan Athens, he used their own culture to point them to God and then Jesus.

Both approaches were great, because they demonstrate Paul's understanding, compassion, and love for his audiences. Paul's approach at Mars Hill has left such an impression that Mars Hill has become a popular name for new churches in post-Christian secular America.

Our approach should vary depending on our audience. If you are going to minister to college students, you need to speak their language and understand their world. If you are going to have a community church in the suburbs, you need to know and have an answer to the challenges facing families and

---

[105] Matthew 22:36-40
[106] 1 Chronicles 12:32
[107] Daniel 1:17

what matters most to those in your demographic. If you are going to be a missionary in Mauritania, there is so much to know, you better get started right away! In John 4:35, Jesus said to look at the fields as they are ready for the harvest. The Greek word[108] "to look" means to study, to analyze, or to contemplate.

My wife, Lynette, has a real eye for New York City culture. She knows fashion and trends, and, more importantly, knows why women's hearts in this culture have been broken repeatedly. This ability "to look" makes her effective in her mission field.

These are no small needs we face today. They require work, diligence, and a commitment to study and pay constant, careful attention to ever-changing cultures. I have found that some Christian groups focus exclusively on the gospel, while others focus primarily on culture and becoming culturally relevant. I believe it is our calling to embrace both the message and culture around us to see the gospel transform individual lives and culture, to the glory of God.

Where is God calling you? What do you know about that culture? Is that based on generalizations, or are you confident it is true? What type of ministry will have the most impact?

The good news is that if you will take some time, listen to the people, and try to understand where they are coming from, God can use you in any culture around the end goal is not cultural relevance, but significant spiritual transformation. Without prayer and understanding your cultural context, it may never happen.

Why is this so? Because love communicates in all cultures, through all languages, at all times. When you love people, you give your best to understand them and add value to their lives. When this happens, doors will open to share the gospel.[109]

---

[108] If you are interested the word is theaomai.
[109] Luke 10:1-9

All full-time ministers need ongoing training in Bible and theology, leadership, practical ministry skills, and cultural and contemporary issues, but you do not have to wait for the training to pursue your calling. Instead, you should build training into your calling.

Training can come through a variety of sources. You will receive most of your training through practical experience. You will receive it as you become a lifelong learner through reading and studying. You will receive training through mentors, pastors, and coaches along the way. You may also receive training through formal education and seminaries.

The key is to continue in training, keeping your mind and heart hungry for the rest of your life. As we can see in the verse from the beginning of the chapter, Timothy's mentor challenged him to live this way. He could challenge him, because Paul lived that way, himself.

One of the last things Paul wrote to Timothy was, "bring my books."[110] His list of credentials is impressive; apostle, writer of much of the New Testament, mentor, master theologian, extraordinary missionary, and miracle worker. And fortunately for all of us, he kept learning 'til the end.

---

[110] 2 Timothy 4:13 (NLT)

7

THE COST OF
OBEDIENCE

"Whoever wants to be my disciple must deny themselves, and take up their cross daily and follow me. For whoever wants to save their life will lose it, but whoever loses their life for me will save it."
Luke 9:23,24

Have you ever heard that if you follow Jesus, you will have perfect peace and all your problems will go away? Sounds good, doesn't it? It might sound good, and we might want it to be true, but it is not what the Bible says. And it certainly does not hold true to the historic experience of people who have loved and served God. There is a cost to follow Jesus.

There was a young pastor and teacher in Germany. His country was in upheaval, and many of the people were hurting. In this context, a leader of staggering proportion emerged. His name was Adolf Hitler. As the Nazis grew in power, we all know they tragically and brutally murdered six million Jews. Many forget how they also intimidated and manipulated the churches and their leadership. Those who resisted were either killed or thrown into prison.

The young pastor Dietrich Bonhoeffer helped to form the Confessing Church in Germany, a group that boldly resisted and spoke out against the Third Reich when so many other Christians shamefully compromised and endorsed the Nazis. Taking up his cross daily and following Jesus ultimately cost Bonhoeffer his life, but before he died, he wrote a book that has become a classic, The Cost of Discipleship.[111] He did not just write about the cost, he paid it. He trusted Jesus' promise that in losing his life, he would be saved. Bonhoeffer's story is only one in the long legacy of those who paid the

---

[111] The main premise of the book is the difference between "cheap grace" and "costly grace". Bonhoeffer draws from the Sermon on the Mount, and there are also clear allusions to Paul's discussion of worldly sorrow and godly sorrow in 2 Corinthians 7:8-13.

ultimate price of their lives for their faith in Christ. Many of these are described in detail in another classic, *Foxe's Book of Martyrs*.[112] I first heard about this book when I was a freshman involved with InterVarsity Christian Fellowship.

A few years later, I was spearheading a new campus ministry at UNC Chapel Hill, and I asked one of our new believers to give a brief talk to our group. He was a student athlete (a tough wrestler, an ultimate-fighter type), and, since I was mentoring him, I wanted to give him the opportunity to minister to others. It was something he seemed to be good at, since he had come to this newfound faith in Christ.

I asked him to speak to our young campus ministry (this can be nerve-wracking, as you are never quite sure what a new believer will say). It was right before

Christmas, so it seemed fairly safe. I convinced myself it would be fine—he would give us a nice Christmas encouragement of some sort, the students would be blessed, and he would have a great chance to grow closer to Christ in the process.

What actually happened next was beyond belief. He did not bring Christmas cheer—he spoke on the topic of martyrdom. It was not what any of us expected during the Christmas season and all the typical "baby Jesus" talk.

I will never forget that night. His message on martyrdom was a surprise, but turned out to be excellent and showed from Scripture and *Foxe's Book of Martyrs* how the early church was often built upon the willing sacrifice of the lives of martyrs.

It used to be easy to separate dying for Christ from our contemporary culture and the world in which most of us live. However, with graphic YouTube videos of Christians being brutally martyred in the Middle East, we are, once again, aware that martyrdom is a reality of the Christian faith. From

---

[112] Written by John Foxe and first published in 1563, the book details the accounts of Christians who were killed because of their love for Jesus. The focus is primarily on the early church, but it does give some medieval church history and follow stories of martyrs to the time it was written. It was more than 2,300 pages in its first form, but has been slimmed down considerably, and most versions today are small, paperback editions.

the earliest days of the church, this was part of what it meant to be a disciple.

According to tradition, all of Jesus' twelve disciples were martyred; history tells us that they tried to kill John, but he would not die, so they exiled him on the island of Patmos, where he eventually passed away.[113] Some died at the hands of the sword,[114] others were run through with the spear,[115] and, according to some accounts, Peter was crucified upside down at his own insistence, because he felt he was not worthy to die like Jesus.[116]

We may not be forced to pay that price, but many of our brothers and sisters around the world are.[117] Martyrdom continues to be a part of what it means to follow Christ in the world today. The Pew Research Center lists 145 countries where Christians face harassment or worse – 145!

At the time of this writing, in Israel, yet another Palestinian Arab Christian was martyred in Gaza because he was a dedicated, evangelistic businessman for the cause of Christ; he was a prime example of one willing to take a stand for the gospel in a region hostile to the gospel.

Though we will not likely be called to martyrdom, it would not be the worst thing that we could endure. As hard as it may be to grasp, the Bible describes it as a sign of great faith.[118] It is easiest to understand this lifestyle as a gift or a grace that God gives to some. That is how some of God's servants can go with their families and live in extremely dangerous places, sometimes paying the ultimate price.

He gives them the grace to do it—it does not mean that He wants all of us to rush out and throw ourselves in harm's way to prove our devotion. The story of Steve Saint and Jim Elliott, portrayed in the film The End of the Spear, is a moving and powerful example of this kind of grace. Following Jesus unto death has always proven to change the world.

---

[113] For a detailed analysis of the fate of the apostles, see Sean McDowell's book The Fate of the Apostles.

[114] Acts 12:2

[115] With the obvious exception of Judas, but he died early, too.

[116] Foxe, John, Foxe's Christian Martyrs of the World. Uhrichsville, OH: Barbour and Co, 1989, 7

[117] There is an organization, "Voice of the Martyrs," that works to prevents and put an end to this cruel practice. You can find their website at www.persecution.com.

[118] Hebrews 11:35-38

This kind of grace in action, and this extent to which people love and follow Jesus, always changes the world. The story of Stephen (found in Acts 7), the first Christian martyr, was a dramatic turning point for the early church. It is also the only time in Scripture [119] that we see Jesus stand up from His throne to receive one of His followers.

Very soon after Stephen's death, one of those witnessing and even relishing in that barbaric moment had a divine appointment with the resurrected Lord Himself. He was dramatically converted and went on to change the world. Saul of Tarsus was his name. We know him today as the apostle Paul.

Whether or not God gives us the grace to pay the ultimate price is not the issue. The issue is that all of us are called to pay the price of obedience. The cost of discipleship is one of obedience. If we are to serve Jesus, we must obey Him. Obedience will always cost us something. I have seen this principle demonstrated
again and again.

A close friend of mine and partner in ministry was called to the full-time ministry as an international student at UNC Chapel Hill. He finished three master's degrees, got married (his wife finished her Ph.D.), and returned to his homeland of Taiwan, where they both accepted teaching positions at a prestigious university.

In 1995, when he joined me on a trip to China, the Spirit of God began to move in a powerful way, and he was reminded of the call to ministry God had given him. He knew he had to respond to the call, but he did not know how to tell his wife. They were starting a family, they both had great jobs, and ministry in China meant danger, uncertainty, and none of the privileges afforded university professors in a free nation.

Reluctantly, he told his wife about the direction he felt God was leading them. At first she said, "No way." However, she gradually came to see that this was where God had called them. When they told their parents, they faced even more opposition: his in-laws threatened to disown them if they went.

---

[119] Acts 7:55, 56

My friend could not deny that God was calling them, and they needed to obey. Through prayer and patience, setbacks and adversity, they endured and God began to turn hearts and open doors in powerful ways.

They left the security and stability of their home to join God in a great adventure. They have participated in a miraculous move of God of historic proportions in China—it is no exaggeration to say their lives have influenced multiple thousands, if not tens of thousands of Chinese. Even their nationally distinguished parents from Taiwan have grown to recognize this calling and have given God glory, as they have been reconciled with each other and once again walk in family harmony.

All of this came at a great price – sacrifices, facing fears, leaving security, not having parental approval, and much more. Through the years, I have come to recognize in their story and many others that there are three costs that typically follow the call to full-time ministry. I can sum them up in three words: peers, parents, and pressures.

1. PEERS

In the world of young people, support structures are primarily formed from peer groups. Some sociologists[120] have argued that, for the majority of young people today, the formative influence of peers has surpassed even that of the nuclear family.

If an aspiring full-time minister has a diverse group of peers, chances are good that most them will not understand or support the decision for ministry. Even if most their peers are believers, they probably still will not "get it."

I will never forget how one of my peers told me (when I explained my calling), "I'll do anything I can to stop you." Years later, he came to me and asked how he could join me.

Jesus' own circumstances can provide great comfort. Matthew, Mark, and Luke[121] all include the story of Jesus' mother and brothers interrupting Him

---

[121] Mark 3:31-32, Matthew 12:46-47, and Luke 8:19-20

[120] Dr. Ron Taffel's book, The Second Family: Dealing with Peer Power, Pop Culture, the Wall of Silence – and Other Challenges of Raising Today's Teens in an extensive, explicit, and fascinating study in this subject.

as He is teaching in the temple. They called Him outside to speak with Him, presumably because they were not too sure what He was up to. The Gospel of John takes it to the next level. Early in His ministry, the Bible flat-out states that Jesus' brothers, "did not believe in Him."[122]

One of Jesus' strongest supporters was His cousin, John the Baptist, but, as John was sitting in jail, he sent his disciples to Jesus to communicate that he was now doubting whether Jesus was truly who He said He was.[123] Even though Jesus Christ was the Son of God, He still had human emotions, and this doubt from his friends and family had to hurt.

There are other passages that show the people of Nazareth (His hometown) doubting and questioning the validity of Jesus' calling.[124] We do not see any of His peers rushing to His defense. At His most difficult moment in the Garden of Gethsemane[125] the only support He could rely on was His Heavenly Father. This is, no doubt, a model for us to follow.

Additionally, all the disciples had similar circumstances where they refused to cave in to the pressure of their peers and made a resolute decision to follow Jesus. As the old hymn says, "though none go with me, still, I will follow."[126]

2. PARENTS

It can be hard on a parent to understand why their honor student who just spent tens of thousands of dollars on a degree will not use that investment in their career. If the parent is not a believer or has had a difficult experience with church, the thought of their child becoming a minister may cause them to feel left out or ostracized.

---

[122] John 7:5

[123] Luke 7:18-20

[124] Luke 4:21-22

[125] The disciples feel asleep three times when Jesus asked them to pray on the night He was arrested. They took
off when He was arrested and tried, and they went back to their life of fishing after He died.

[126] From the Hymn "I have decided to follow Jesus" written in the 1880s. The story that inspired the him can be found at http://thecripplegate.com/why-we-sing-i-have-decided-to-follow-jesus/

This can be extremely challenging, but, when it is handled with love and guidance, it can turn out to be a great blessing for all. In my case, my Jewish father thought I was nuts for wanting to be a minister. Yet, he became a follower of Christ and my biggest fan.

Another factor to consider is the new breed of parents today. Whether you call them, "Little League Dad," "Soccer Mom," or "Helicopter Parents," they are constantly hovering over their kids. They are hyper-involved in the lives, choices, and futures of their children.

My friend, Dr. Tim Elmore (the Founder and President of Growing Leaders, Inc.),[127] recently told me about a parent who was irate that their child received a "C" on a paper in a class in college. It turns out that the reason they were so upset and wanted to engage the professor was because the parent wrote the paper!

As it becomes increasingly common for parents to live vicariously through their children, the stress on relationships between parents and sons or daughters going into full-time ministry will, undoubtedly, increase.

Becoming a minister is not in the plans for most parents as they dish out thousands of dollars for their child's education. It was not in the plans for my oldest son, either, but that is what happened. After finishing his master's degree from the University of Edinburgh in Scotland, he decided to give his life to missions and full-time ministry, which he continues to this day.

Anyone who finds themselves in this tense situation should view it as an opportunity to show the love of Christ and honor their parents. It can be a great moment to develop patience and perseverance, as it takes time for them to accept it.

They may not see how the ministry utilizes many of the skills that a degree provides, even indirectly. Ministry will not provide the biggest salary, and may not give them prestigious bragging rights among their peers, but, as God moves in your life and ministry, I believe they will, eventually, honor your obedience to the call.

---

[127] Growing Leaders is a fantastic organization that is dedicated to developing young leaders who will transform society. You can find out more about them at www.growingleaders.com.

I have seen it happen time and again. It worked that way for me.

3. PRESSURES

All of us face pressure in life, but full-time ministry takes pressure to another level. It is constant, beyond your control, affects more than just you, and the consequences are eternal.

William Carey-- a famed Baptist missionary to India—is known as the Father of Modern Missions. Take his life for example, as told by Edmund Clowney, "Every conceivable obstacle seemed to block Carey's obedience: objections from his friends, the reluctance of his wife, her long illness and death, the powerful and planned opposition of the East India Company, the disinterest of those whom he sought at such vast sacrifice to reach."[128] Probably the worst part of all was the opposition he faced from his Christian friends who did not believe in missions as a calling.

The variety of pressures runs along a wide spectrum. From finances to spiritual warfare, from standing with a suffering family to coaching an addict to freedom, from praying for a miracle to hearing horrific and heart-wrenching details that you would give anything to forget, the pressure *never* ends.

This pressure and fear can be especially difficult for single women. Some people are unsure of the validity of women in ministry even today, and it can be a lonely, difficult road. But God is using heroic young women who are responding in obedience and entering full-time ministry.

Answering the call to ministry is not always fun, exciting, or even spiritual. It can be grueling, excruciating, and painful. That is why it is important to understand it is a calling that requires obedience. As you are reading this book, you can probably recall people in your life who, themselves, withstood this pressure, in order to propel you further in your relationship with God. Their story may encourage you.

---

[128] Clowney Edmund. Called to the Ministry. Phillipsburg, New Jersey: Presbyterian and Reformed Publishing Co., 1964

In his second letter to the church at Corinth, Paul gives a snapshot into what his life of ministry was like:

> Three times I was beaten with rods, once I was pelted with stones, three times I was shipwrecked, I spent a night and a day in the open sea, I have been constantly on the move. I have been in danger from rivers, in danger from bandits, in danger from my own people, in danger from Gentiles; in danger in the city, in danger in the country, in danger at sea; and in danger from false believers. I have labored and toiled and have often gone without sleep; I have known hunger and thirst and have often gone without food; I have been cold and naked. Besides everything else, I face daily the pressure of my concern for all the churches.[129]

That is quite a list. Thank God I cannot say my list looks that bad. It is amazing that of all the pressures that Paul faced, what he came back to, what he concluded with, was the constant pressure of his care for the churches.

If you respond to this call to full-time ministry, you will face pressure. You will have times when you will be persecuted. There will be other times when you feel like you are not making a difference or you have no idea how you are going to work out the finances.

I have found that, in the end, it is caring for and carrying the pain of people that weighs the heaviest. People are why we are in the ministry. It is not for fame or fortune. Most ministers will not get either. God loves people, and He calls you and I to do the same. Remember, some people will disappoint you and break your heart.

Jesus connected ministry with fishing. If I compare my early days in ministry to fishing, I caught a lot of boots and tires. I ministered to one guy for more than a year, regularly spending time discipling him. I was very excited about his growth and progress, as he seemed sincere. But I was wrong. After that season, he decided he did not want to be a follower of Christ or listen to what I had to say. He went on to become a leader in the gay/lesbian campus group.

---

[129] 2 Corinthians 7:25-28, NIV, emphasis mine

Another young man prayed to receive Christ and then quickly developed of lying to me and then betraying me. After a few of months of working with this "new believer," he asked to borrow my car. Since he was taking time off from college to "get his life together," I gave him my keys thinking it would help. He ended up stealing my car. He took it on a joyride across the state for a few days before he brought it back. He must have thought that my car was one of the perks for anyone I baptized. Maybe I should have held him under a little longer.

Yet all the pain, all the horror stories, and all the never-ending pressures seem so small once you see God do something amazing. Eventually, God will use you to bring the Gospel to people, and their lives will be radically changed. You will develop wonderful relationships that grow to become some of the greatest treasuresof your life. The joy I have received from serving needy orphans, desperate house church leaders in nations where the gospel is banned, new believers in our churches, and many other lives I have had the privilege of being a part of, makes it all worthwhile.

There will be moments when people you care deeply for go through devastating crisis and tragedy. You will come to love some who are so likeable, but just cannot seem to get it together, and you will have to patiently endure through their ups and downs. Sometimes, they will not make it. One day, they might just give up and be gone.

You will give your all for people. You will pray, fast, bind and loose, counsel and encourage, and anything else you can think of to help people grow closer to God. You will literally try everything; sometimes, it will become a great testimony. Other times, you will have to file it under "pastoral mysteries file," and you will not have anything else left to say.

In those moments, you may feel tempted to feel like a failure. After all, people look to you to set the captives free. It is your job. It is what you get paid for. Then, you will remember that Jesus did not help everyone either,[130] and you will be encouraged.

---

[130] One of the more chilling details of the account of "the rich young ruler" (Matthew 19:16-26, Mark 10:17-31, and Luke 18:18-34) is how Jesus' interaction with the man ends. Both Matthew and Mark's versions say that "he went away grieving," (Matthew 19:22, Mark 10:22) which isn't exactly the happy ending you'd hope for. Not everyone in the crowds the followed Jesus got healed. And, perhaps more obviously, in the end, Jesus did not save Judas

You will weep with joy in one moment and shed tears of hurt and pain in another. People will make you laugh, cry, cuss (or at least make you want to cuss), shout, steam, and vent. This is the cost of doing life together. It is a high price, but, in the end, you will find that it is worth every tear and every sacrifice. If ministry is your call, nothing else can satisfy you.

8

THE CONSEQUENCES
OF DISOBEDIENCE

"For I know the vast number of your sins and the depth of your rebellions. You oppress good people by taking bribes and deprive the poor of justice in the courts. So those who are smart keep their mouths shut, for it is an evil time. Do what is good and run from evil so that you may live! Then the LORD god of Heaven's Armies will be your helper, just as you have claimed. Hate evil and love what is good; turn your courts into true halls of justice..."
Amos 5:12-15 (NLT)

These are the words God gave the prophet Amos. Amos, in turn, obediently spoke them to the people of Israel. It is not hard to see how appropriate they are, even today.

It is as easy as turning on the news or opening a web browser to see examples of sin, rebellion, and injustice. Whether it is racism in America, destruction in Syria, or child-slavery globally, we can see the effect of sin all over the world. Unfortunately, you can probably see this in your own community, or even in your neighborhood.

When God uses prophets in the Old Testament, they are typically given a message that tells the people of God that change is essential. Naturally, God deals with the character and the calling of the prophet before He sends them to everyone else. After all, no one wants to listen to a prophet who is not practicing what he preaches!

It is interesting to see how God deals with this situation. He fashions a person who then receives a message and tells the people something like Amos said in the verse above.

The right response for the people is not talk; it is obedience. Communicating the message verbally is an important step in the process, but it is usually the action of obedience that creates change, and obedience is the role of the people. The prophet Jonah had to learn this the hard way by living in the belly of the fish for three days. It was a good thing that God told the fish to swallow, but not to chew.

Obedience, however, rarely takes place without someone calling people to repent on behalf of God. Both the message *and* the action are critical. It is not one or the other.

When the messenger of God functions, the people can respond. When each party obeys and does their part, the result is reconciliation between God and an individual, a community, a culture, and even a nation.

What happens if there is no messenger? Paul asked this question to the church at Rome, "How, then, can they call on the one they have not believed in? And how can they believe in the one of whom they have not heard? And how can they hear without someone preaching to them? And how can anyone preach unless they are sent? As it is written: How beautiful are the feet of those who bring good news!"[131]

How can people hear the gospel, if no one is sent to preach it? What happens if no one stands up and calls the people to turn from sin, rebellion, and evil? When will the people run from evil, so that they can live if there is no one to challenge them? How will the courts be true halls of justice, if no one stands up for the victims of injustice? We must have evangelists, prophets, pastors, and leaders to turn our nation to God.

Politicians cannot do this alone. Doctors and lawyers cannot do it either, nor can actors, actresses, or professional athletes. Even committed businessmen who invest and build their communities are not able to do this work.

At least not on their own—that takes a team. It takes a messenger who gives their whole life to communicating God's messages to the people. The foundational member of this team is the man or woman who answers the call

---

[131] Romans 10:14, 15

ANSWERING THE CALL   88   *RonLewisMinistries.org*

of God to bring the teaching of the Word and prayer for the transformation of lives and the equipping of the saints.

From the earliest days of the church in Acts, full-time ministers were highly dedicated and motivated to spend their days, weeks, months, and lives proclaiming the gospel, without the responsibilities of another profession. Paul said, "woe is me if I do not preach the gospel."[132] The cost of disobeying God and not answering his call is missing out on a life lived with Him and taking part in His story of redemption.

In the Gospels, we do not see Jesus give prayer requests often. But, after a long and exhausting day of ministry, when the crowds seemed overwhelming and the needs were innumerable, He said to His disciples, "The harvest is plentiful but the workers are few. Ask the Lord of the harvest therefore, to send out workers into His harvest field." (Matthew 9:37,38)

At the risk of stating the obvious, if Jesus asks us to pray for something, it is important. He emphasizes this point because He realizes there are a lot of sheep with no shepherds.[133] In honor of this verse in Matthew 9, with a daily reminder of their iPhone alerts, global leaders of Every Nation Campus take a minute or more every day at 9:38 a.m. to pray for leaders to respond to the needs of the harvest.

There have been times in history when revivals have started from businessmen and women, people who were not in full-time ministry. For example, the New York prayer revival of 1857 was started by Jeremiah Lampier, a businessman in downtown New York City. His first gathering only had a handful of people, but the prayer meeting grew quickly and became a revival. This revival swept the entire northeast and changed lives, churches, communities, and even cities to the glory of God.[134]

As wonderful as a revival can be, if it is to be sustainable, it must include

---

[132] 1 Corinthians 9:16

[133] If you read the passage that the quote comes from Matthew 9:35-38, you'll realize that Jesus asks for more workers after seeing how the people needed someone to care for them. He compared the situation to sheep and shepherds. That's one of the reasons why you sometimes hear of pastors or ministers referred to as shepherds.

[134] For more on this story read "Revival Born in A Prayer Meeting" from America's Great Revivals, Bethany House Publishers, Minneapolis, Minnesota Originally published in CHRISTIAN LIFE Magazine.

people repenting and turning to Christ. These people will need others to help them become disciples of Jesus. This is a process that takes time.

Years ago, a famous football coach of University of Colorado, Bill McCartney, started a men's movement. Across the United States, huge gatherings of men cried out to God and stood with their friends, coworkers, brothers, and sons, committing to lead as men of godly character. This movement waned due to the lack of local churches and strong leaders who could make disciples out of those caught up in the movement.

Most would agree this is still the case today. Sheep need shepherds, and our cities need changing. We need to ask the Lord of the harvest to send out workers. The statistics are not very encouraging. Dr. Aubrey Malphurs, an expert church consultant, strategist, and professor, laments the verdict his studies reveal. Eighty percent of churches in North America are either plateauing or in decline, and, each year, thousands are closing.[135]

He also comments on the fact that the number of young people going into ministry is also in decline. Citing older source, he states, "In 1975, as many as 24 percent of clergy were 35 years or younger. However, in 1999, only seven percent were 35 or younger, and a growing number of these were women."[136] Church researcher George Barna adds the discouraging news that the "unchurched population" is up 92 percent over the past 13 years.[137]

Despite these numbers, I believe God is pouring His Spirit on a new generation. Many of you reading are a part of this new generation, and you will make a great impact on many people. I believe a door of opportunity is open to us, if we will cling to the cross, break free from our addiction to self, and rise up to serve Jesus with all of our being.

There was a time when this nation was sending thousands of missionaries all over the world. Today, missionaries are coming from all over the world to evangelize the United States. Thank God for their obedience to the call,

---

[135] Malphurs, Dr. Aubrey. A New Kind of Church: Understanding Models of Ministry for the 21st Century. Grand Rapids, MI: Baker Books, 2007, 18.

[136] Malphurs' footnote comes from, Elis, Tiara. "Christians Meet to Discuss the Scarcity of Young Minsters." The Dallas Morning News, September 14, 2004 edition, p. 5B.

[137] Malphurs, Dr. Aubrey. A New Kind of Church: Understanding Models of Ministry for the 21st Century.

but we still need those who will, themselves, answer this call and give their time and full attention to prayer, the preaching of the Word, and ministry to others.

People from every nation should be cultivating and calling forth full-time ministers. This is happening in many student centers on every continent. The challenges are great, and, yet, the power among God's people is greater.

There is no shortage of darkness in the world today. As Edmond Burke said, "The only thing necessary for the triumph of evil is for good men to do nothing."

The power of pornography is growing at an exponential rate as it becomes increasingly accessible. What used to shock us—whether it is graphic violence, filthy language, or explicit subject matter—now barely catches our attention.

If this is going to change, God's people need to respond and call others to hate evil, to run from it to what is good.

And what about justice? There are more people suffering in the bondage of slavery today than at any other time in recorded human history.[138] Even though every nation has anti-slavery laws, there are still 45.8 million victims of modern slavery according to Gary Haugen, the Chief Executive Officer of International Justice Mission.[139] It is now easier to engage in slavery than ever before. In 1850, a slave in the Ivory Coast would have cost the equivalent of $40,000. Today, you can purchase one for roughly $30.[140]

According to the Department of Justice, the fastest growing form of slavery is human trafficking: trapping, forcing, and transporting people into inescapable and inhumane bondage.[141] According to the most recent reports, 600,000 to 800,000 people are victimized every year, and trafficking is the third most lucrative form of international crime, behind drugs and

---

[138] Llewelyn Leach, Susan. "Slavery Is Not Dead, Just Less Recognizable." The Christian Science Monitor, September 1, 2004 edition. http://www.csmonitor.com/2004/0901/p16s01-wogi.html Site accessed January 7, 2008.
[139] Ibid.
[140] Ibid.
[141] Ibid.

weapons.[142] Eighty percent of the victims were female, and seventy percent of them were sex slaves.[143]

Here is the most heinous, shocking, and demonic part of this tragedy: right now, there are more than two million children in the commercial sex trade.[144] Children who try to help their family through working honest jobs are often tricked and kidnapped, and they wake up in brothels, where they are habitually raped, while their captors get rich.

What could be a greater injustice? Could there be anything more evil than that? Imagine how this makes God feel. Along with many others, Lynette and I have had many sleepless nights because of this atrocity. Where are God's prophets, demanding that this evil stops? We need to ask the Lord of the harvest to send workers.

What about the millions who die every year because they lack clean drinking water? Where is the response to the genocide in Syria, the compassion for displaced refugees from terrorism and civil unrest, the answer to the global orphan crisis, and the commitment to stopping the AIDS epidemic? If the government had all the answers, the needs would have been met long ago.

Who will cry out for justice, love, and compassion out of service for God? Isaiah heard the triune God say, "Who will go for us?" Isaiah answered, "Here I am, Lord, send me."[145] We need to ask the Lord of the harvest to send workers.

Preachers, ministers and full-time workers can influence culture. They can be a part of a social revolution. It has happened before, and it can happen again. Saint Patrick brought education, literacy, and the life-changing power of the gospel, forever changing Ireland.

John Knox, generally regarded as the founder of the Presbyterian denomination, was the moral compass for England and Scotland during his lifetime and regularly challenged and influenced the questionable practices

---

[142] Ibid.
[143] Ibid.
[144] According to UNICEF, by way of the International Justice Mission. www.ijm.org.
[145] You can read this entire exchange in Isaiah 6:8, especially in the NASB or the NLT..

of Mary, Queen of Scots. She was famously quoted as saying, "I fear the prayers of John Knox more than all of the assembled armies of Europe."

Though he is best known for writing the classic hymn, "Amazing Grace," John Newton was also the captain of a slave ship. In time—because of what God did in his life through his faith in Christ—he willingly left the lucrative, yet deplorable, business for the full-time ministry. One of the men he pastored, British politician William Wilberforce, is generally credited as being the driving force behind ending the Atlantic slave trade.

The only minister who signed the Declaration of Independence was John Witherspoon. As the president of the College of New Jersey (today known as Princeton University, which, as we mentioned earlier, was founded on Christian principles), Witherspoon helped shape the political views and thinking of many influential American leaders—including the fourth American president, James Madison. His influence continues in this nation today.

God used a Canadian-American man named John G. Lake so dramatically, to heal the people of Spokane, WA, that the government declared it the healthiest city in America.[146] Although he passed away long ago, his apostolic faith mission of South Africa continues to bear fruit today.

We all know of the work of Dr. Martin Luther King, Jr. for the gospel and social justice, but it is easy to forget that his work started in a pulpit and that he often quoted the Bible, claiming that his source of inspiration came from above.

For more than forty years, Agnes Gonxha Bojaxhiu loved the poor, the sick, and the orphans of Calcutta. The world would come to know her as Mother Teresa, a woman whose dramatic love for God and people changed the world. This lifestyle is at the heart of what it means to be a follower of Christ. Her legacy inspired author Anthony Walton to challenge the Body of Christ with a powerful goal. "Imagine a million-strong army of Mother Teresas and the impact that would have on the neighborhoods throughout

---

[146] (Forward). Lake, John G. Diary of God's Generals: Excerpts from the Miracle Ministry of John G. Lake. Tulsa, OK: Harrison House, 2004, v..

planet earth"[147]

These revolutionaries changed their cities and nations because they obeyed. Who knows how the darkness may have triumphed, had they had disobeyed and not answered the call.

The cost of disobedience is too high. Will you pay the price of obedience?

---

[147] Walton, Anthony. Future Church: Church by Design. Wellington, New Zealand: Global Tribe Productions, 2001, 45.

9

FUNDING
THE MINISTRY

*"I thank my god every time I remember you. In all my prayers for
all of you, I always pray with joy because of your partnership in the
gospel from the first day until now . . ."*
Philippians 1:4-6

As men and women wrestle with this calling, perhaps the most prominent issue they confront is finances. If money was not an issue, I think many more people would be in full-time ministry. Financial concerns are a sticky point, a daunting challenge, and often the driving force behind second thoughts and uncertainty.

Although a small minority may view the ministry as being for "money-grubbers," far more view it as a pledge of poverty, ensuring a future of lack. Whether we conjure up thoughts of the ravens bringing Elijah food, a dusty monastery, or horror stories of ministries that need urgent resources in the next twenty-four hours, it is easy to think of full-time ministry as demanding a vow of poverty.

The value of the call is not what is questioned. It is the viability. Few will question the why, since most people will not deny there is, indeed, a need for people to answer the call of God.

It is easy to ask, "how?" The fact is we *should* ask this question, even though there may be uncertainties that accompany the process of getting answers.

At the same time, it is true to say that, with every vision that comes from God. He brings His provision. Financing the ministry is His responsibility, and the God we serve owns the cattle on a thousand hills.[148]

---

[148] Psalms 50:10

The provision may not become visible exactly when or how we expected it, but, if you are in the will of God, His blessing is coming. As the apostle Paul wrote to his partner church at Philippi, "My God will meet all of your needs according to the riches of His glory in Christ Jesus."[149] He is able to do immeasurably more than than we can ask or imagine, according to His power that is at work within us.[150] God's provision is something we must understand biblically. God wants to provide for His work. As a matter of fact, He wants to provide extravagantly for His work.

When Moses was collecting the offering from the people of Israel for the tabernacle, he had to tell them to stop ". . . because what they already had was more than enough to do the work."[151]

When Jesus fed the five thousand, [152] He started with five loaves of bread and two fish. After five thousand men had eaten (not to mention all the women and children who, assuredly, would have outnumbered the men), there were twelve baskets of leftovers. This was no fluke. Jesus later fed four thousand[153] (again, just counting the men) with seven loaves and a few small fish—this time with seven baskets of leftovers. You know it is a supernatural meal when you feed thousands of people and finish with more leftovers than what you had when you first rang the dinner bell!

This process of believing for financial provision will stretch you, challenge you, encourage you, and, in the end, cause you to fall deeper in love with a God who will appear more loving and generous than you could have ever imagined. That has been my story, and it has been the experience of so many who have walked down this same road.

Speaking about this subject to the church in Corinth,[154] Paul writes that a soldier in the army does not pay his own way, a man who plants a vineyard receives the fruit of the vine, and the shepherd benefits from the sheep.

---

[149] Philippians 4:19
[150] Ephesians 3:30
[151] Exodus 36:6-7
[152] Matthew 14:13-21
[153] Matthew 15:29-38
[154] 1 Corinthians 9:7

Drawing on the custom and arrangement that God made with the Levites he continues:

"Don't you know that those who serve in the temple get their food from the temple, and that those who serve at the altar share in what is offered on the altar? In the same way, the LORD has commanded that those who preach the gospel should receive their living from the gospel. . ." 1 Corinthians 9:13, 14

Notice that it does not say, it is a good idea, or maybe they should, or this is the way it has always been. No, it says, **"the Lord has commanded . . ."** Any time you see that phrase, whatever comes next is guaranteed to happen—whether or not we agree or understand. When God commands something, you can count on it.

Soldiers do not pay for their own expense in any army. When I think of the thousands of soldiers selflessly serving around the world, I am relieved to consider that they, at least, get paid to be there. Likewise, "soldiers in God's army" get their provision from their commander-in-chief. It is His great desire to provide for those who would follow Him with their whole lives and their careers in His mission on earth.

Let us consider three basic ways people can finance their full-time ministry calling.

1. HIRED TO WORK FULL-TIME

The first practical option for many going into ministry is to be hired and paid by a church, ministry, or non-profit organization. Depending on the size of the ministry, this is often done by invitation or through development within the ministry into full-time employment.

Some larger organizations have recruiting, advertising, and an open and formal application/hiring process. These organizations are more corporate in nature, sometimes having a human resources department and an extensive hiring process.

It is my experience that most churches and non-profits hire from within, through established relationships or their volunteer base. In a sense, the relationship functions as the first part of the interview process. When you know someone and have a prior relationship with them, a necessary amount of trust and confidence creates a good starting point for employment.

I have initiated employment opportunities with friends and members who are proven, effective, and "gung-ho" for our organization. Hiring people like this sure beats relying on the want ads in popular Christian magazines or website job lists.

If you believe God has called you to full-time ministry in the church or organization you are currently a part of, my advice is to proceed prayerfully and set up an appointment with a proper representative. When it is time to consider employment, the following are questions that you should ask of yourself and others:

- *Do you know the leadership structure? Is there an organizational chart?*
- *Is there an actual offer on the table?*
- *Is there a job description?*
- *Is there a salary? Health care? Other benefits? Do you have to raise support?*
- *Does the organization have a human resources department or an employee manual?*
- *Is there room for growth and development?*
- *What has been the experience of other employees?*

Oftentimes, people make the mistake of viewing a church or ministry as something so holy that it would be wrong to ask these kinds of practical questions. As someone who has hired many people, let me encourage you to recognize that this is not the case. It is appropriate to ask these questions, and, with the right heart and a good attitude, there is nothing unholy about it at all. Providing for yourself and your family[155] is very important to God, and vocational ministry can be part of the provision, when you approach it with wisdom and your eyes wide open.

---

[155] 1 Timothy 5:8 tells us that anyone who does not provide for their immediate family has denied the faith and is worse than an unbeliever. Ouch.

Although most ministries will not have the corporate infrastructure of Deloitte (where my wife worked for years), most of them will be able to provide the answers you need to have clarity and understanding.

In turn, you should expect that the ministry or church will have certain professional expectations of you, as well. It is not enough for them that you read your Bible some, pray for a while, and hang out with people while you drink a latté.

When you enter the ministry, you commit to do a specific job that should include performance evaluations based on a job description and achieving certain results.In turn, the non-profit agrees to take care of the basic aspects of your livelihood and well-being through a fair wage.

One translation of 1 Timothy 5:17,18 explains this concept, "Elders who do their work well should be respected and paid well, especially those who work hard at both preaching and teaching. For the Scripture says, 'You must not muzzle an ox to keep it from eating as it treads out the grain.' And in another place, 'Those who work deserve their pay!'" (NLT)

Other translations state that these elders[156] —or ministry leaders— are worthy of double honor, while The Message paraphrases double honor as "give a bonus." The idea is clear that, indeed, the workers deserve their pay, and, even though they are servants, their service should not come without appropriate and reasonable compensation.

The New Testament letters are also filled with qualifications and expectations of the one who serves.[157] They include guidelines for leadership, including: a history of responsibility (often demonstrated as a husband and father), the fruit of the Spirit (self-controlled, patient, loving), and a mature and humble attitude.

If the characteristics listed in these passages are not present in one's life, the discussion of full-time ministry should be put on hold until these issues are

---

[156] "Elder" is a title that the Bible uses for a leader or overseer in the church or among the people of God.
[157] Titus 1:7-9, 1 Peter 5:1-3, and 1 Timothy 3: all give excellent descriptions of church leadership and ministry responsibility.

settled. One cannot stress enough how critical these character issues are to sustainable ministry success.[158] The man or woman who meets these criteria, who has been called of God to the ministry, and is effectively carrying out his or her work, is certainly worthy of a salary.

2. PARTNERSHIP TEAM

Another proven financial support method that allows people to respond to this calling is the designated partnership team. Many missions and parachurch organizations are well-known for this approach. Cru, Youth with A Mission, Overseas Mission Fellowship, Young Life, Chi Alpha, InterVarsity Christian Fellowship, Every Nation Campus, and many other missions organizations follow this method.

The partnership team refers to a group of individuals who are committed to the vision and mission of the person they are supporting, and demonstrate this commitment through financial investment. In the great tradition of the Levites and the ministers in the book of Acts, this allows the "missionary" the provision to follow God's call with their full time and attention. As difficult as it may be to grasp, Jesus, Himself, had a partnership team, as referenced in Luke 8:1-3.

Paul's letter to the Philippians gives us a window into the fact that Paul had this kind of relationship with the church at Philippi (Philippians 1:5, 4:16). The language of "partnership in the gospel," "gift(s)," and "you sent me aid again and again when I was in need" all come straight from this epistle.

Paul writes that the gifts and blessings that the generous Christians sent him as a result of their partnership created a credit to their accounts that pleased God. Simply put, the letter from Paul to the Philippians was, on one level, a partnership thank-you letter. Because this is Scripture, we know that these are not just the words of a grateful minister, but that they demonstrate a partnership model that God blesses in order to strengthen His church and to accomplish His mission on earth—that of releasing more workers into the harvest.

---

[158] James 3:1 states that not many should attempt to be teachers of the word, because those who do will be judged more strictly.

The faithfulness and integrity of organizations that follow this model, along with humble and heroic missionaries, have helped this "Philippians model" gain recognition and acceptability in the larger body of Christ. One of the great results of this has been new opportunities for more missions groups to follow this pattern.[159]

Training for partnership development is available in abundance. For example, Steve Shadrach's book, *The God Ask,* is a comprehensive tool for those who wish to excel in this season of partnership development. As Shadrach says, he is "no fool" and would be "afraid to launch into any ministry endeavor without [his partnership team]."[160] If this is your path to the ministry, check with your organization or leadership. They will give you the expertise available to help you succeed in this path.[161]

As you walk through this process, it is normal to be nervous and somewhat uncertain, but it is clear that God promises He will meet all of your needs.[162] Most people are surprised at how the Body of Christ will support and stand with them, in order to share the fruit of the ministry.

If this is the call of God, you *can* do it! Remember, when God gives vision, He brings provision.

3. PART-TIME EMPLOYMENT/CREATIVE ENTREPRENEURSHIP

In Acts 18, the writer includes an interesting detail about Paul during one of his missionary journeys. He meets a Jewish man named Aquila, whose wife is Priscilla. They would become some of his most faithful partners in ministry.

---

[159] ECFA Accreditation is a good way to ensure and maintain standards of church and mission organizations. Their seven standards are as follows: doctrinal issues, governance, financial oversight, use of resources and compliance with laws, transparency, compensation-setting and related-party transactions, and stewardship of charitable gifts

[160] Steve Shadrach, The God Ask, loc. 207.

[161] For more than 20 years, our ministry, Every Nation Campus, has trained multiple hundreds and managed multiple thousands of partners to assure best practices, integrity, and a successful relationship between missionaries, partners, and the organization.

[162] Philippians 4:19 is the promise noted; however, the condition is that this is God's will for one's life.

Verses 2 and 3 state, "He came to them, and because he was of the same trade, he stayed with them and they were working, for by trade they were tent-makers."[163] The Bible does not reference this again, but, apparently, Paul generated income at different times through different means. In Philippians, we clearly see the partnership model, but, here, it seems that Paul worked at least some of the time to generate the resources he needed for his missionary work. This is why this method is often called the "tent-making" model. I know of many ministers who, out of necessity to take care of their families, do creative entrepreneurial ventures or work part-time.

In my early years, tent-making was my strategy, as the young church I was starting was unable to provide a salary to meet my needs. In most situations, I view this solution as temporary. The Scriptural pattern is clear that ministry requires focus and dedication, and Paul reminds us that those who do the work should be provided for. As he says, "Don't muzzle the ox while it's treading."[164]

Is God primarily concerned with oxen in this passage? No, what He is saying is that one should not keep the full-time workhorse from the resources and sustenance they need to keep going strong.

Still, at times, creative entrepreneurship is what a person must do, to make ends meet. It can be a terrific funding mechanism, as long as it does not compete with your ministry, nor create a conflict of interest. I realized a long time ago that I could not be ministering and pastoring people, while, at the same time, trying to get them to buy my products. It does not work, and it potentially creates a conflict of interest and a question of ethics.

While there are many creative solutions that those who are called to ministry do to enable them to go into full-time ministry, these three are the most common, and they will serve many people who are entering ministry well. When an individual earns his or her living doing ministry as their profession, believe it or not, even some governments are favorable and

---

[163] Acts 18:2,3
[164] 1 Corinthians 9:9

supportive of them. The IRS currently offers two tax benefits to individuals who are engaged in ministry. Your church can guide you through the process of being "commissioned" or licensed, which is a necessary step to receive both benefits.

You have the choice to request exemption from paying into Social Security and Medicare. This is available if you have a "conscientious objection" to receiving public assistance funds from the government. This is not a light choice to be made for financial incentive, but out of your personal convictions. This decision should be made after thorough consideration of the options and long-term impact. You will probably want to consult an accountant, as well. This exemption only applies to income you receive for ministry work.

The church organization can designate a portion of your income as housing allowance. The portion of your salary approved and used for reasonable housing expenses is non-taxable from your federal income tax. The allowance includes rent or mortgage, utilities, and other expenses. There are limitations to this benefit; please review with a member of your church's leadership team.

The result of both benefits is that men and women in full-time ministry can use the maximum amount of their resources to invest toward the pursuit of God's mission.

Do not make legal and accounting decisions based on my information, alone. My goal is only to let you know these kinds of benefits may be available to you, depending on your job status and the organization you work with. Seek guidance from a qualified non-profit tax specialist or professionals in the non-profit organization you wish to serve. As you proceed in discovering your calling, seek the best counsel available. Speak to your pastor or pastoral team at length. If you have leaders over you, they are there for your good and protection. As they give you the "green light" to press toward the full-time calling, pursue it with all you have to give.

Remember this encouraging word from Scripture, "And God is able to bless you abundantly, so that in all things at all times, having all that you need, you will abound in every good work."[165] He is "the Lord who will provide."[166] That is His name.

---

[165] 2 Corinthians 9:8

[166] In Genesis 22:14, when the Lord provided a ram for Abraham so he didn't have to sacrifice his son, Abraham named that place, "the Lord will provide," or in Hebrew, "YHWH Jireh," a name that people still use to refer to God.

10

REWARDS OF
FULL-TIME MINISTRY

*"I have fought the good fight, I have finished the course, I have kept the
faith; in the future there is laid up for me the crown of righteousness,
which the Lord, the righteous Judge, will award to me on that day . . ."*
2 Timothy 4:7, 8 (NASB)

There is no way to describe the joy that comes from knowing you have done
what God has asked of you. As Jesus said, "My will is to do the will of Him
who sent me and to accomplish His work."[167] If there were no other rewards,
the knowledge that you have fulfilled what God has asked you to do is more
than worth it.

Recently, I was meeting with a mega-successful multi-millionaire
businessman. He and his wife were pouring their hearts out to me, wondering
if they had truly hit the mark with their lives. They, like countless others,
were longing for purpose that riches and fame cannot satisfy. We had a
wonderful discussion, and my respect for them grew, because they were
so down-to-earth, transparent, and humble. I longed to help them find new
vision and new life as they began the process of living for others and giving
their lives and resources away.

As Paul was growing older and preparing for his graduation to heaven he
said, "I have fought the good fight, I have finished the course, I have kept
the faith; in the future there is laid up for me the crown of righteousness,
which the Lord, the righteous Judge, will award to me on that day . . ."[168]
Paul had a sense of his obedience to the Lord and the future reward that was
coming. His boast was not his ministry and all the things he accomplished.
He was excited that he had kept the faith and finished his course.

What is your course? Are you finding it? More importantly, are you fulfilling

---

[167] John 4:34
[168] 2 Timothy 4:7, 8 (NASB)

it? As you do, your rewards will surely come. If not in this life, then in the life to come.

If there were no other rewards, finding and fulfilling His will for our lives would be more than enough. The world longs to know this secret.

Before we describe some of the other blessings, let me be clear. When you get down to it, there are no unique rewards for becoming a minister. There is no Bible verse about a reward for going into full-time ministry.

There are, however, rewards for being obedient to His calling on your life. This is what we are after—obedience to His perfect will.

Becoming a doctor or lawyer because of a sense of direction from God can bring the rewards of obedience. Being an actor or actress who wants to bring God to Hollywood, Bollywood, or Dollywood may be the calling on your life. Your obedience to God is what He will reward.

My dear friend and gospel partner Peter Kim (the name is changed for obvious reasons) is doing extraordinary and often dangerous work for North Koreans. I stand amazed at how he can continue to do what he does for the Lord. There have been times when his life was literally on the line and in grave danger. Gospel work may not have the Jason Bourne look and feel, but it is often more exciting than fiction. It is opportunity met with challenge.[169]

Peter and I worked together for many years at my home church, King's Park, in Durham, North Carolina. We prayed and dreamed of finding a way to help the North Koreans living in the worst circumstances imaginable. Satellite images at night reveal that North Korea is physically the darkest industrialized nation in the world. This is certainly symbolic of the spiritual darkness rampant in that nation.

Finally, after years of ministering together in Durham, the door of opportunity opened. The Lord beckoned Peter and his young family. His reward was not in responding to a need, but answering the call of God. Hundreds of North

---

[169] Check out 1 Corinthians 16:9. The idea that there are open doors but many adversaries sounds to me like it could apply to either ministry or international espionage.

Koreans have been saved and rescued through Peter and his team from that evil regime.

For most of us, if we tried to do his calling, we would either be imprisoned or martyred. Martyrdom is not my call for today; I am sure my wife and children would agree! But Peter does what he does with ease. Certainly, he will receive the reward of the Lord. He has made more sacrifices than we can imagine, but he never complains, and he does it with a sense of true fulfillment. He is in his "sweet spot." He is obedient, as Paul said, "to the heavenly vision."[170]

In the words Oswald Chambers, "The only way to be obedient to 'the heavenly vision' is to give our utmost for His highest— our best for His glory."[171] Chambers' devotional, *My Utmost for His Highest* has inspired millions over the years. This devotional has been like a friend's counsel to me many times.

Beyond the reward of obedience, God, our Heavenly Father, also gives temporal blessings, tokens of His grace as we go along in obedience. God is a good, giving, encouraging, and rewarding God.

As I have worked beside and observed those in full-time ministry, three consistent blessings mark most of their lives—people, places, and possibilities for impacting the world.

1. PEOPLE

Through the call to the ministry, you can be privileged to meet some extraordinary people. It is amazing how God opens doors for us to meet with people from virtually every walk of life. Ministry does that. There is no room for prejudice or partiality in ministry. The founder of the Methodist Church, John Wesley, has commonly been quoted as saying the world was his parish.

---

[170] In Acts 20:24, Paul says that his life is worth nothing, and his only aim is to finish the race and complete the task the Lord has given him. In 26:19, he tells King Agrippa that he was not disobedient to his vision from heaven.

[171] This classic line comes from the March 11th entry: Chambers, Oswald (author) Reimann, James (editor). My Utmost for His Highest. Grand Rapids, MI: Discovery House, 1992.

Most of us in ministry have had meaningful interaction and care for orphans, the homeless, and the "powerless" of the world. This is dear to my heart. I have also had interactions with a President of the United States, senators, Congressional leaders, business leaders, billionaires, major movie producers, professional athletes, and everything in between. Encounters with some of these people have occurred in some unlikely places. From discount stores to the seat beside me on an airplane, to sharing a ride on subways, to vacation destinations, God is always putting me where I need to be.

I will never forget the time I met one of the NFL's most influential head coaches. I do not mean to be crude, but he was standing next to me in the restaurant bathroom, and, in that moment of awkwardness, the Lord prompted me to give him a word of encouragement. It was a providential moment, and he joined our dinner party for the next few minutes, just to show his gratitude.

One amazing night at the historic Lamb's Theatre in New York City, I met the man I consider the finest person I have ever known. His name was Harald Bredesen. Harald was eighty-four when we met, and he died when he was eighty-eight. He was just amazing—a true leader of leaders and a pioneer in a move of God. His life touched millions. For nearly four years, he poured into my life and provided things that had never been there before. He inspired me in ways too deep for words.

He taught me to love on a deeper level and to laugh at the little things in life. He mentored me in prayer and ways to connect with God. What a gift he was! He came at the right time, a God-appointed time, and it was an eternal reward that marked me forever.

Your ministry calling will, likewise, put you before many people. I remember one time overhearing a tired minister say, "I like everything about the ministry but the people." People can be wearisome, but, at the end of the day, they are such a great reward. And there is no ministry without them.

Enjoy them. Love them. They are your calling.[172]

---

[172] Matthew 9:35-38 describes Jesus' heart for people that was at the center of His ministry, and it demonstrates how He sees the primary reason for more workers: taking care of the people.

2. PLACES

The call to ministry can literally take you around the world. To my great surprise, I have ministered in and been to the African plains, the Great Wall of China, the Pyramids of Egypt, the Austrian Alps, and many more exotic locales. Each of these places has brought a special reward from the Lord. God has met with me in all of these places and countless others.

It is not always some huge "ministry" moment, either. Sometimes, God just wants to show you His love and give you moments which will mark you and touch you in a real way. For example, once on a prayer mountain outside of Seoul, Korea, I had a profound experience, wherein God healed my heart and renewed me for years to come.

Another time, my son, John Luke, and I were invited to go backstage during the *American Idol Gives Back* live telecast in Los Angeles at an iconic theater. On one of the biggest episodes of one of the most popular television shows in America, we were hanging out with great musicians, singers, and bands backstage. Imagine how excited we were to be invited into their dressing room of one of our favorite bands? God knew that would be a gift we would love and remember for a long time. On this occasion, it was just a moment to enjoy with my youngest son.

There are times when God wants to give you something special to show you how much He loves you. It might be an amazing experience, a hard-to-find item, or a once-in-a-lifetime trip, but, when you receive it, you will know He did it just for you.

My heart here is to encourage you that the ministry is a calling to adventure, not a job to endure. God wants you to enjoy life, experience joy, and, by His grace, get the job done![173] The world is dying to see men and women who know their purpose, decide to live it without restraint, and make a lasting difference because of it.[174]

---

[173] Nehemiah 8:10

[174] Daniel 1:18-20 tells us that the king of Babylon found Daniel and his friends to be ten times better than their peers. The main reason was these four young Hebrew men, even as they lived in a foreign, ungodly land, obeyed the Lord, and, as a result, God blessed them.

3. POSSIBILITIES

Finally, through pursuing the Lord in full-time ministry, we are given amazing potential to change lives and impact the world. We are called to find solutions and answers. One of the ways the Lord can reward us is through using us to find solutions to real problems.

In 1998, I was asked to visit several underground pastors of a large nation. With my friends Taylor Stewart, Kara Reed Waddell, and others, I went to a secluded city in the interior of the country. The van ride, itself, was quite rewarding, as we were with some very special leaders who led millions of believers.

We were driven to a remote building. We could feel the excitement in the air, but we did not know what was going to happen. It turned out that we were privileged to join a historic meeting. Several key leaders from the underground house church network had gathered for prayer, unity-building, and strategy. They specifically wanted to meet with us to express their gratitude for our labor in helping establish many training centers for their educational needs.

It was a humbling moment. Everything in me wanted to scream out, *"You are the heroes! You are the ones putting your lives on the line!"* They had all been tortured and imprisoned for the gospel. It was such a deep reward to have this time with them. I will never forget it.

Possibilities typically involve one person at a time, and, initially, they do not often occur on a grand scale. When I met Ann, she was a confused college student trying to find her way. She had eating disorders, depression, and coped with a great deal of anxiety, having grown up without a father. I shared Jesus with her, and she became a Christian after three Bible studies.

Through the love of God, Ann's life started to come together, and peace came to her in lasting ways. She was delivered from all her eating disorders. She was able to focus on her relationship with God, her medical career, and, in time, her husband and family. For years, she was a faithful part of our ministry, until her career moved her to another city.

Over the years, she would consistently show up on one special Sunday in June—Father's Day. She did not say it at first, but, after a few years, I figured it out—Ann was coming in order to quietly say to me, "Happy Father's Day." Is there any better reward than this?[175]

Full-time ministry is often portrayed as a lifestyle of drudgery and sacrifice. While it certainly can have its moments, it has been my personal experience and that of so many of my peers, that it consistently offers unique and often extraordinary rewards. These rewards go beyond the perks of so many other careers, things not measured in monetary ways.

You may not get rich as the world counts riches, but you will, undoubtedly, experience a wealth that no retirement fund, bonus program, nor worldly recognition can match. We live in a society in which people are desperate for fulfillment on the deepest levels. If you are called and, then, experience the deep satisfaction that comes from pursuing and fulfilling that call, what a testament to the world you will be.

If you are pursuing the call and mission to full time ministry, you will discover what Israel's beloved King David experienced: "Surely goodness and mercy will follow me all the days of my life."[176]

---

[175] When I realized that's how she felt, it reminded me of 3 John 4. Here, in his old age, this great man of God reflects that there is no greater joy he has known than when young people he has mentored love and obey God.

[176] These are David's words in Psalm 23:6. Clearly, this promise is not specific to those in full-time ministry and is available to all of us. I mention it to show that, contrary to popular opinion, those of us in full-time ministry are not exempt from goodness and mercy! And thank God for that.

EPILOGUE

I hope you have enjoyed this book. Here are my final thoughts.

I sincerely believe God will order your steps.

Scripture promises:

"The steps of a man are established by the Lord, And He delights in his way.

When he falls, he will not be hurled headlong, Because the Lord is the One who holds his hand." [177]

If your heart is with the Lord, you will not miss his will. He is going to open and shut doors, and you will find peace in how God operates by the Holy Spirit and, at times, through circumstances. Please do not be discouraged. His will is going to be accomplished, and the process you are in right now is all part of His plan.

May God bless your every endeavor for His glory.

Ron Lewis

---

[175] Psalm 37:23-24

CPSIA information can be obtained
at www.ICGtesting.com
Printed in the USA
BVOW10s0758190217

476520BV00003B/9/P